AF445806

REMINISCENCES
OF
AN ARMY NURSE
DURING
THE CIVIL WAR

Adelaide·W·Smith
Independent Volunteer

DEDICATION TO THE
BOYS IN BLUE

1861-1865

and to those brave women who, with smiling faces and breaking hearts, sent them forth to save their country and their homes, while they themselves toiled in fields and elsewhere, waiting to welcome home too many who never returned; and to that band of heroic devoted women, many of whom left luxurious homes for the discomforts and privations of hospital life, and died, self-sacrificing patriots of the war, this true story is affectionately dedicated.

NATAL PUBLISHING LLC
ARS LONGA, VITA BREVIS

Copyright© 2024 Natal Publishing

All rights reserved

1831   1911
Adelaide W Smith

CONTENTS

Foreword

This story, devoid of literary pretensions, is a simple narration of day-by-day experiences, as they came to me, during five years of volunteer work in hospitals of the Civil War.

At the risk of some slight repetition, it has been thought best to include "Recollections of Lincoln" and "Love in Camp" practically as they were when published separately.

I wish to express my high appreciation and thanks for the confidence and encouragement of those friends who thought the book should be written that the younger generations may know something of the work done by women during the war.

To the Rev. W. M. Brundage, of Brooklyn, I am especially indebted for practical suggestions that have made the publication possible.

With some limitations, during two summers, I betook myself to the unique Seventh-day-Baptist University town of Alfred, New York, where the story was written on the picturesque campus, in a pure atmosphere free from all disturbing elements.

It has been a labor of love and pleasure to review the old scenes, replete though they were with suffering and death, for the thought of the comfort we were able to give to the "Boys" and the remembrance of their gratitude remain. In no other benevolent work of my life was the reward so immediate and so inspiring as in this ministration. I have given real names and literal words as nearly as possible, except in cases where there was something unpleasant to relate; and I may truly add that, even to be young again, I would not have missed those years of incessant care and anxiety, given in the hope of saving brave soldiers for their country and their homes.

A. W. S.

CHAPTER I
A View of the Situation

"Heartstrong South would have his way
Headstrong North had said him nay,
They charged, they struck; both fell, both bled;
Brain rose again ungloved;"
    *   *   *   *   *

SIDNEY LANIER, Centennial Poem.

It is not my intention to write history, but it seems advisable to mention in a few brief notes or extracts, for the benefit of the present generation, the sentiments held during the Civil War.

When the first Confederate shot was fired upon the United States flag, then floating over Fort Sumter in Charleston Harbor, many months of unrest, foreboding, and apprehension of a coming terror were experienced by the people of the North. This fatal shot caused the separation of hitherto devoted families; fathers and sons were arrayed against each other, some in hate, some in sorrow; and even mothers, wives and sisters shared this unholy animosity. All took pronounced sides with North or South, except the "copperheads," whom all loyal Northerners despised.

General Winfield Scott, the hero of many a hard fought Mexican battle, though quite superannuated, was still in command of the United States armies. Imperative, supercilious, an austere disciplinarian, usually adorned with all the ornamentation of his rank, with chapeau and white plumes, he was, especially when well mounted, a conspicuous figure, quite justifying his sobriquet of "Fuss and Feathers."

GENERAL WINFIELD SCOTT

In consequence of the secession of South Carolina, on December 20th, 1860, General Anderson, commander of the forts of the harbor of Charleston Bay, evacuated Fort Moultrie six days later.

The "Star of the West," bringing reinforcements, was fired upon by the Confederates, thus preventing the landing of United States troops.On April 11th, 1861, General Anderson refused an order to surrender to General Beauregard, who, during the 12th and 13th, ordered a furious bombardment from the surrounding forts upon Fort Sumter. Being unprepared for the attack, General Anderson was compelled to capitulate and to take refuge, with his garrison, on ships outside the harbor. On April 14th, 1861, however, he saved the National flag, which is now carefully preserved in the Museum of the War Department at Washington, no casualties having occurred.

The fort was held by the Confederates till the evacuation of Charleston, February 17th, 1865.

On April 14th, 1865, General Anderson had the happiness to raise the old flag once more, with his own hands, over the demolished fort.

The following extracts from an unpublished letter of John White Chadwick were selected and kindly given me by Mrs. Chadwick.

SOME EXTRACTS FROM AN ACCOUNT OF A TRIP TO CHARLESTON AND BACK ON THE OCCASION OF THE RAISING OF THE FLAG ON FORT SUMTER AFTER THE CIVIL WAR

"Land, ho!"

When at last it was permitted us to raise this cry, we were indeed a happy company. We entered into the experience of Columbus and Cabot and Balboa. The pilot came on board. He told us, as the pilots always did, to come to anchor, and we obeyed him. And lying there on the still water, in the perfect air, there came another feeling than that of joy. The atmosphere grew heavy with deep thoughts and wonderful associations. Our hearts were softened and our eyes were dashed with sudden tears. In dark and lurid splendor, all the great events of four long, painful years rose up before us. And then again we hoisted anchor and steamed slowly up toward the city in the deepening twilight...................

The war ships, lying there like terrible grim monsters,

manned their rigging as we passed, and cheered us lustily. But there was something in our throats forbidding us to answer them with equal heartiness.

Passing under the battered walls of Sumter, we sang with trembling voices, "Praise God from whom all blessings flow." And to the left was Wagner and the ditch where Colonel Shaw was buried with his dark but trusty men.

It happened so, that God in His great mercy, permitted us to be bearers of great tidings to the city—news of the rebellion's virtual end to this community which saw its mad beginning. Once shouted from our deck, it flew from wharf to wharf, from ship to ship, and was received with shouts of thankful joy. The night shut in over the accursed city as a band upon the wharf played the dear strain "America." It was a time never to be forgotten, pregnant with thoughts that must remain unspoken. Before I tried to sleep I stepped ashore, and, just for a moment, standing there under the silent stars, thanked God that He had punished awful sin with awful retribution............

On Friday, just after ten o'clock, we started for the fort in the steamer "Golden Gate," which the Government officials kindly placed at our disposal. About the fort the scene was at once beautiful and exciting. There were thirty ships and steamers in its immediate vicinity, and they blossomed all over with flags. And the little boats belonging to the war ships were shooting here and there and everywhere, obedient to the lusty strokes of their stout oarsmen, dressed for the occasion in their very best.

We were on shore by half past twelve o'clock, and wandering at will about the tattered mound that had once been Fort Sumter. Indeed they had made "Ossa like a wart." It had no form or comeliness. It was a perfect heap.......... Anon came General Anderson and Mr. Beecher and the rest. The General's speech was, for so great an hour, the very smallest possible affair. But when it came to raising the old flag he did hoist away like a good fellow, and it went up right handsomely. The people rose up as one man, and shouted their hurrahs as if they thought to wake the echoes from the St. Lawrence to the Gulf. And the band played "The Star Spangled Banner" just as if they meant it,—as they did of course. And then from ship and fort the cannon thundered away like mad.......... And when they ceased with their roar Mr. Beecher took it up and thundered, to good purpose, for an hour or more..........

Saturday saw William Lloyd Garrison preside over an assembly of two thousand colored people, if not more, in Zion Church, and noble words were spoken which these people did not fail to understand.........

From Charleston wharf to Hampton Roads our voyage was pleasant, and the weather very fine........... Going into Hampton Roads, on Tuesday, swiftly and silently over the still water, we saw a vessel with her colors at half mast. Not long after a pilot shouted to us across the waves, from a great distance, that the President was dead. Either we could not or we would not believe it.

Another vessel sailed along with drooping colors and told us *how he died.* And then the shadow of his death swept down and folded from our sight all of those great and rare experiences which we had been enjoying. It seemed to us that we should never be able to recollect them from that shadow. We went ashore at the great fortress, where his dear feet had been, scarcely a week before, but we had no eyes to see anything..............

It had been proposed to go to Portsmouth, Norfolk and to City Point. But we had no heart for it. And so we came together in the cabin and voted that we would go home.

JOHN WHITE CHADWICK

The Government called for seventy-five thousand troops on April 15th to put down the rebellion "in ninety days," according to Secretary Seward's confident announcement.

On April 19th, the Sixth Regiment of the Massachusetts Brigade, first to respond to the call, was fired upon by a mob while passing through Baltimore, and a number were wounded and some killed.

The Ellsworth Zouaves were enlisted chiefly through the enthusiastic patriotism of young Colonel Ellsworth, who, on arriving at Alexandria with his regiment, saw a Confederate flag flying above a small hotel, and at once ordered the flag hauled down. This was refused, and the indignant boy rashly rushed to the roof, and dared to pull it down himself, when he was shot dead by the rebel owner. Colonel Ellsworth was killed May 24th, 1861. Lincoln's grief at the death of this daring boy was overwhelming. Ellsworth had studied law with him for a time in his office, and he loved him as a son; and as a son and early martyr of the war, he was laid in state at the White House for funeral services.

War with its untold horrors had begun.

Meanwhile it was becoming evident that President Buchanan had permitted, or had at least become strangely blind to the introduction of foreign ammunition into Southern ports, while the traitor Secretary Floyd, still under oath to the Union, held his office until the last possible moment, encouraging and assisting the South in building forts and, in many ways, accumulating almost openly materials of war.

At last the people awoke to the fact that many southern regiments and garrisons were well equipped for the conflict, while the unsuspecting North was almost wholly unprepared. People had become so accustomed to "fire-eaters' bluster" and their threats and boastings of the superior prowess of the South that, if they listened at all, it was considered mere political bombast which passed unheeded until war was actually begun.

In November, 1861, General McClellan superseded General Scott, who then retired from active duty, at the age of seventy-five, and died later at the good old age of eighty.

General McClellan began a slow thorough system of discipline, which was very trying to the enthusiasm of volunteer recruits, who soon discovered that to use the pick and shovel were as essential duties as carrying a musket, and were now compelled to work in swamps and trenches throwing up earthworks and entrenchments for many long months.

The impatient public claimed that egotism and ambition prevented General McClellan from moving "on to Richmond," thus prolonging the war, and his army settled down before the enemy "in masterly inactivity." During this time many disgruntled soldiers climbed hills and trees and saw the city of Richmond practically defenseless "for three days." Still he did not move. This large army had lived and worked in earthworks for many weary months, until malaria and dysentery had sent hundreds of incapacitated soldiers North to be cared for. They were among the first bitter fruits of the terrible struggle scarcely yet begun.

GENERAL GEORGE B. MCCLELLAN

Not long after the defeat at Bull Run—Manassas,—both sides claimed the victory,—did we for a moment believe that Southern courage was equal to Northern valor in an open conflict, or that the rebellion could not be put down within a few months; and so we stood aghast when the attack under General McDowell failed to put down the rebellion in a single battle.

General Horatio C. King, in his address before the thirty-seventh reunion of the Army of the Potomac, repeated these potent words of General Grant:

"As I recall the interview General Grant spoke in substance as follows: 'I cannot imagine why any one should conceive for a moment that I would not be glad to work in any capacity with General McClellan. I have known him but little personally since we served together in Mexico, but I have always admired him both as a man and as a soldier, and I am probably under greater obligations to General McClellan than to any one man now living. General McClellan was called to a great command, unfortunately for him too early in the history of the war, when many difficult military and political questions remained unsettled. He and his acts were the subject of wide discussion and unjust criticism, but General McClellan was the man who created the great instrumentality with which I had the honor of closing out the rebellion. General McClellan organized, trained, disciplined, led, and inspired the Army of the Potomac. General McClellan made that army the finest fighting machine of our day, if not of any time. It was his good work in creating that army which enabled me in my turn to accomplish the things for which I received the glory, and for all of which I am grateful to General McClellan.'"

CHAPTER II
Long Island College Hospital, Brooklyn

In July, 1862, one hundred and twenty-five patients from the Army of the Potomac were sent to the Long Island College Hospital. No adequate preparation had been made to provide for these sick men. Through the press a public call was sent out for volunteers. Many ladies and gentlemen at once offered to help care for the sick, and to supply food for their emaciated bodies.

An endorsement of the distinguished physician of Romson Street, Dr. Burge, made me quite happy by affording me the privilege of helping to care for the soldiers in our city.

Among the large number of our best Brooklyn people to volunteer their help and support was our saintly Mrs. Richard Manning, who continued her ministration throughout the long duration of the war, and for many years after gave substantial help to the destitute families of soldiers; and also Mrs. Anna C. Field, chief organizer and president of the Woman's Club, as well as of the Woman's Suffragist Association. Both of these clubs celebrated, during the spring of 1909, in the new Brooklyn Academy of Music, the fortieth anniversary of their organization. I believe that, in modern Brooklyn, no other woman has done so much, in her long life of benevolence and charity, as this Mother of Brooklyn Clubs, for the elevation and encouragement of women especially in ethics and literature.

Watches of four hours each during the day were assigned to the women, and at night the same number of hours were allotted to men volunteers.

Owing to the astonishing liberality of the citizens of Brooklyn, the hospital donations seemed like a great cornucopia overflowing the larders of the improvised kitchen. Tender, motherly care, combined with the best of diet, at once restored many a poor, hungry homesick boy. Most of them recovered and returned to their regiments or were sent home.

MRS. ANNA C. FIELD

My first patient was a bright, cheerful young man, Allan Foote, of Michigan, who had been dangerously wounded by a shot that passed through the left lung and out at his back. Such wounds were then supposed to be fatal. He was, however, convalescent, and later was discharged. When he returned to his home in Michigan he again enlisted, raised a company, and went out once more to the front as captain. This time he served till the end of the war, when he returned to his native State safe and well.

ALLAN FOOTE

A lady, wishing to say something flattering of him to a visitor, remarked: "Why, he was shot right in his back." Seeing the boy wince at this innocent imputation, I explained that he had received that shot in the breast while facing the enemy in battle.

Among many incidents of his early army life, Allan Foote told me the following:

"I shall never forget his expression when my father gave his written consent to my enlistment in the army in April of '61, as he handed it to me and said, while tears were running down his cheeks, 'My son, do your duty, die if it must be, but never prove yourself a coward.' We can hardly imagine at what cost that was given, and it is now a source of much satisfaction to me to know that God in His mercy so guided me while in the service that no action of mine has ever caused a pain to my father's heart, and when I returned at the close of the war he seemed as proud of my scars as I was."

John Sherman was a remarkable case of lost identity. He was eighteen years of age, six feet in height, with broad shoulders and a Washingtonian head, and seemed like some great prone statue as he lay perfectly helpless but for one hand,—a gentle fair-haired boy to whom we became much attached. He was evidently refined, and perfectly clear on religious and political subjects. Though without a wound he had been completely paralyzed by concussion caused by a cannon. He could take only infants' food and drank milk, which was all the nourishment he could retain. The mystery was that he claimed to come from Cattaraugus County, N. Y., but when I wrote letters to every possible locality, nothing could be learned of such a boy; nor could the officers of his regiment trace him during this time. Some scamp who claimed to come from his town, was admitted through the carelessness of the hospital attendants, and so deceived the poor boy that he gave him ninety dollars army pay just received, to send home to his father. Of course the scamp was never heard of again. My theory is that he enlisted under an assumed name and town, and had, after the concussion, forgotten his real name and identity. He was sent to the Fifty-second Street hospital, where I saw him a year later, walking alone and quite well,—a finely developed physical form. Though he knew me, he held to his old statement. Later he was cruelly persuaded to ask for a discharge which left him homeless, with no refuge but the poor house.

Soldiers' homes were then unknown; and I fear that, at

least for a while, he was cared for as a pauper. About this time I went to the "field work" and lost sight of him, though I have often wondered what his fate has been.

A miserably thin, gaunt boy, whom we knew as "Say," came under my observation. He was never satisfied, though he ate enormously, and whenever we passed through his ward he invariably shouted: "Say! ye ain't got no pie nor cake, nor cheese, nor nuthin', hev ye?" When he reached home, his father, a farmer, sent to the hospital the largest cheese I ever saw. This the men all craved; but it was a luxury denied them by the doctors. Patients often had it smuggled in. One poor fellow was found dead, one morning, with a package of cheese under his pillow.

As the "L. I. C. H." was a city hospital, emergency and other cases were often brought in. A pathetic case was that of a little boy about six years old, who had been run over by a street car. As he lay, pale and mangled, awaiting the time to have his leg amputated, his mother, in broken English, crooned and mourned over the unconscious child, saying, "Ach, mine liddle poy, he will nefer run mit odder poys in the street and haf not any more good times." I saw that the child would not live through the operation, and tried to comfort the poor mother while it was going on. When the mutilated, stark little form was returned to her, her grief knew no bounds, though she still believed he would revive.

In another ward poor Isaac was slowly dying of dysentery, gasping for a drink of cool water, which the rules of the profession at that day denied to such patients. Day after day he lay helpless, while a large water cooler dripped constantly day and night before his feverish eyes and parched body.

One day he called to me and said: "Won't you please sit on my cot so I can rest my knees against your back? They are so tired and I can't hold them up,"—poor fleshless bones that had no weight. Somewhat relieved while I sat there he went on: "Now, Miss Smith, you think I am dying, don't you?"

"Well, Isaac," I replied hesitatingly, "we fear you are."

Then with all the strength of his poor skeleton body, he exclaimed, "O then, give me a drink of water that I may die easier. You know I am dying, so it can do no harm."

ADELAIDE W. SMITH, 1863

Could I refuse a dying man a drink of water, even in the face of orders? He wanted "just a pint." Watching my chance I went quickly to the cooler and brought a glass of cool water.

With unnatural strength he raised himself and, reaching out for the glass, grasped it and swallowed the water with one great gulp. Then returning the empty glass he cried: "There, that was just half! O, give me the other half." This I did, rather fearfully. After greedily drinking the water he dropped back with a sigh of relief, saying—"Now I can die easy." I arranged quietly with my patients in the ward so that he could have water as long as he lived; but not many days after I found his empty cot.

The hospital, at that time, was little known, being quite obscured under the limitations of two conservative, retrogressive old doctors, who showed no favor or sympathy for the sick men, and seemed to see them only as probable "subjects."

Many just protests from the kindly women workers were utterly disregarded by these doctors. Dr. Colton, a handsome young man then an interne, though not of age or yet graduated, found himself often between the "upper and nether millstones" of the urgency of volunteer workers, and the immovable, implacable heads of the hospital. Dr. Colton, now a successful retired physician, occupies a prominent position in this hospital which, in late years, is ranked among the very best of Brooklyn's institutions.

Meanwhile the people grew tired of the continual demand for supplies, toward which the hospital contributed very little, though it drew regularly from the government "rations" in the form of thirty-seven cents per day for each man. Consequently public contributions became very meagre.

Then in the autumn came ninety-one sick and wounded soldiers, who stood—or dropped—on the grass plots surrounding the hospital while waiting to be enrolled. A procession of grey skeletons, they were ghastly, dirty, famished, with scarcely the semblance of men. One of them stared at me rather sharply and, seeing that I observed it, said, "Excuse me, ma'am, I haven't seen a white woman before in many months, an' it seems good to look at you."

It became difficult to get proper food in the hospital for the men. Some of the volunteers, like myself, could still give their whole time and thought gratuitously, and we continued bringing supplies from our homes for special cases. My mother sent gallons of shell clam juice,—the most healing of all natural tonics when boiled in the shell,—which became popular in the hospital. My mother also invited companies of four or five convalescents at a time to "a good square meal," when they always chose for their suppers, coffee, buckwheat cakes and sausages. Two gallons of batter would become hot cakes; and it took the combined help of the whole family and the cook to keep them supplied; but the hungry boys were at last satisfied and happy. I had no difficulty in obtaining passes for them, as they felt in honor bound to return promptly to the hospital.

One poor fellow, dying of typhoid, was so irritable and profane to the ignorant, heartless men-nurses of the hospital, that they would not care for him during the night. Realizing that the end was near, and feeling certain that he would otherwise die alone, I decided one night to remain with him until his last breath. Just before he died, even while the pallor of death overspread his face, he struck at the nurse whom I had compelled to stay near to help him. At last the poor dying man gasped: "Lift me up higher! higher! higher!!" We raised the poor skeleton as high as we could reach,—and it was all over. His family refused his body, saying, "He was no good to us in life, why should we bury him?" It is not difficult to imagine that his home influences had been unfavorable to the development of moral character.

Clancy, then a fine looking, kindly policeman, had waited to take me home near morning, as he did on other occasions of this kind.

Some months later, being almost the only young woman still visiting the hospital, I felt obliged to report to that rarely good man, Mr. McMullen,—whose benevolence and generosity had at first brought the patients to the hospital and to the care of the people,—the neglect of soldiers, who were then treated like charity patients. He immediately reported these conditions to the medical department, and the men were removed to the government hospitals, which were by this time systematized and in good running order.

After the patients had been transferred from the Long Island College Hospital, I secured a pass on the steamboat

Thomas P. Way, to visit hospitals of the "Department of the East," in charge of Surgeon McDougall, a thorough disciplinarian, and a just, kind man.

David's Island, on the Sound, had a finely conducted hospital, with a diet kitchen in charge of ladies. There I saw hundreds of well-fed, happy Confederate patients, so many, indeed, that they could not be supplied at once with proper clothing, and so made a unique appearance as they walked about in dressing gowns, white drawers, and slippers. They were soon to be exchanged for our own poor skeleton "Boys" who were coming home slowly and painfully, some dying on the way, to be met by kindly hands and aching hearts eagerly awaiting them.

Fort Schuyler Hospital, on the East River, was formed like a wheel, the hub being headquarters and the spokes extending into wards for patients. One young man of much refinement had been at one of our home suppers, and afterwards the company made a pact that if we were alive one year from that date we should hear each from the other. He exclaimed—"Dead or alive, you shall hear from me!" Being a spiritualist he believed this possible. He was sent to Fort Schuyler and one month later died of small-pox. At the appointed date and hour a year later, I thought of this pact and tried to put myself in a receptive state. I did not, however, see him nor feel any manifestation of his spirit.

CHAPTER III
Bedloe's Island (Now Liberty)

A number of influential ladies of New York City had formed a society named "Park Barracks Association." By permission of the Mayor, barracks were put up in the City Hall Park for temporary accommodation of soldiers. But of that particular work I knew very little. These ladies had, however, extended their benevolence to Bedloe's Island. They had, somehow, heard of my work, and a committee waited upon me with an invitation to accompany them, by the Thomas P. Way, on its regular trip to the department hospitals on the river, including Bedloe's Island, three and a half miles down New York Bay, where they wished me to take charge of their "diet kitchen." Fort Wood still stands on one side of the island, little changed since 1862. At that time twenty wards were filled with about eighty patients.

The first floor of the square brick building on the New York side was used as a dispensary, and the diet kitchen was also located here. On the second floor were the quarters of sick officers, occupied at that time by only one officer who had been wounded at Antietam. Comfortable rooms on the third floor became my apartments.

Each lady had a different opinion concerning the management of the kitchen, and urged the wisdom of her particular plan. I soon discovered, however, that Surgeon Campbell, in charge of the hospital, had been so annoyed by the irregular work of these ladies, that he had threatened to close the kitchen. Small wonder, when a different lady came each week and spent most of her time in undoing the work of her predecessor! They were extremely anxious to have me take charge at once, but I asked for twenty-four hours in which to consider, though my mind was already made up.

This being a volunteer work, I wrote the next day, saying that I would take charge of the kitchen on one condition—namely, that I should have no interference or direction from any member of the Association. This they thought rather severe, but it was my ultimatum. They were glad to accept my terms, however, in order that they might continue their benevolent work on the island.

SURGEON CAMPBELL

The day after I took charge, Surgeon Campbell came into the kitchen for inspection and stood aghast at the "confusion worse confounded." I was standing on a chair in a closet, throwing in heaps on the floor endless packages from the shelves. I laughed at his despairing expression, and said, "Doctor, do not expect any order within three days, till these incongruous piles are classified." There were shoes and cornstarch, "trigger" finger gloves and dried apples, shirts and beans, "feetings" and comfort bags, and so on ad infinitum.

The clothing supplies I now separated from the food donations, and had them sent up to my rooms, where, later, the men came with their demands, or with written orders from the ladies, one or more of whom came every day. I soon discovered that, owing to a lack of system, some of the men had succeeded in getting four shirts instead of one; but I concluded that they were four times colder than their warmer-hearted comrades.

At last out of confusion came order. With the help of Surgeon Campbell I planned a printed list, lacking only the addition of the date, name of surgeon, and number of ward to which were to be added each day's orders. I went over this at night, frequently adding extras, and in the morning it was sent to the different wards when the ward masters came for breakfast. The doctors then selected the proper diet for their patients, and the list was returned before ten o'clock.

Four detailed soldiers acted as cooks and helpers. Andrew, a practical, kindly Scotchman, became head cook; and altogether we were much gratified by our good fare. Our success along this line was made easier by liberal government supplies, and the generous donations of the Association, which gave me "carte blanche" for special cases. Our system worked admirably. When the dinner bugle sounded, the ward masters ran with their trays and pails; the first in order calling out his ward number as he entered. I read aloud from one of the twenty lists, which varied slightly each day, and were kept hanging in a row. For example:

"ORDER FOR SPECIAL DIET
U. S. Convalescent Hospital
Fort Wood
 1863
  Ward ....Dr. ....
Dinner, Supper, Breakfast, Remarks
  Tea...........
Cocoa................
Coffee................
Etc., etc.

Ward....coffee for 6, tea 5, chicken 7, roast beef 10, whisky punches 5, egg nogs, etc."

The cook served meats and vegetables, one served tea, coffee or milk in pails, while I managed the jellies, stimulants, etc. We soon reduced the time of distribution for eighty patients to fifteen minutes.

When Surgeon McDougall, in charge of the department, came with his staff to inspect our kitchen, they waited till all was served to the ward masters, and then he said: "Miss Smith, you have the best conducted kitchen in the Department." Having had little experience in cooking, this was a very pleasant surprise. The inspection was continued by a member of the staff passing his white-gloved hand over the range and sides of the iron kettles, etc., which the men kept so clean that they left no trace. The men were also made happy by the approval of the inspectors.

In addition to this we made large puddings for the twenty wards, ten each day being all that our ovens could hold.

At the suggestion of Surgeon Campbell, a courteous Scotch gentleman and strict disciplinarian, I wore a dress of officers' blue with infantry buttons, medical cadet shoulder straps with green bands and gilt braid in the centre.

The Thomas P. Way came daily at 10 A. M. bringing ladies of the Association and many other visitors. Andrew had learned to make "perfect cocoa," which I had served to the guests in my rooms, where, from the large windows, they enjoyed the fine view of Long Island, New Jersey and New York shores.

"LIBERTY"

This was before the days of "Liberty Island," which later was made immortal by the gift of the French people and the great sculptor Bartholdi, whose heroic statue was to have been completed for the great centennial fair of 1876. Failing to accomplish this in time, he sent to Philadelphia the arm holding the torch which now lights the bay, and is a well known signal light to incoming vessels. While in Philadelphia, attending the exposition, with seven friends I climbed the narrow ladder in the arm, and all were able to sit in the circle of the great torch, now upheld by "Liberty."

DAILY ROUTINE

Each morning I awoke at George's call—"Ha'f-a-pas-seex." Andrew would send up a good breakfast for two, as there was always some lady friend or one of my younger sisters to keep me company at night. No other woman except the wives and friends of the officers at the fort were allowed to remain on the island. The cooks soon learned to manage the men's breakfast without me.

At eight o'clock A. M. a dozen or more men came to my door with orders from the ladies for underwear and many comforts. George, who did the work of a chambermaid, having cleared up my reception room (I did my own sleeping room) I then descended into the kitchen and immersed myself in the work of making jellies and other delicacies, while I had four disabled soldiers preparing meats, vegetables, etc.

At ten A. M. came the boat, bringing guests for luncheon, when we had officers, sisters of charity, clergymen, and friends of the patients to entertain, all of whom needed advice or a pleasant word. This caused many interruptions; but was a pleasant break in the monotony of hospital life.

The visitors left on the four P. M. boat. I then inspected the various wards and discovered many delinquencies on the part of the men nurses of which the patients were afraid to complain. Occasionally there was time for a walk around the sea wall, and then came the men's supper at five P. M.

At six dinner was served in my reception room for my friends and myself, and Andrew insisted upon its being a good one. After that officers and their ladies sometimes called.

When the wind howled and the waves dashed high against the sea wall, we could see the twinkling lights of the city while we sat talking and resting till "taps." Then came George to attend to his wonderful coal fires in very large open grates, which never burned low or dropped ashes on the bright polished hearth. His greatest reward was a pleasant word about the fires and he would smile in happiness. Then he brought a bucket of salt water fresh from the bay for my nightly bath, after which we retired to our comfortable cots, where we slept restfully till awakened by the usual "Ha'f-a-pas-seex."

I remember an incident in which human perversity strongly asserted itself. General Wool, then Commander of the Department of the East, sent an order that "No one be allowed to leave the island till further orders." It was suspected that spies were stealing information from the forts. No one was permitted to go even aboard the boat which brought daily supplies.

At once we felt ourselves prisoners, and an irresistible desire to escape to the city haunted me every hour of the day. I was actually planning to elude the guards and to be rowed in a little boat to the city,—three and one-half miles from the island,—when the order was revoked, and I suddenly discovered that I had no urgent object for making the trip.

The post chaplain drew very few to his services. One patient remarked "We can sleep much better in our cots than in the chapel." One Sunday afternoon, after considerable effort, I succeeded in raising a quartette among the non-commissioned officers. I then went to all the wards, urging the men to come to our services, promising them some good old-time hymns. The chaplain was much surprised and gratified at this sudden increase in his congregation, and this improvement was maintained till most of the patients had left the island.

At last orders were read for all convalescents to report to their regiments. This quite emptied the wards and took my staff of domestic helpers. I had a busy time supplying the Boys with necessary articles and luxuries, and "comfort bags" containing sewing material were in great demand! In some of these were found letters that led to correspondence and in many cases to romance.

As the "Way" left the wharf, these grateful men expressed their thanks by rousing cheers to the surgeons and nurses who had taken such good care of them. Then came three more cheers for the kind ladies who had given them so many luxuries and comforting words. Being the only lady present I waved a hearty good-bye for all these kindly women.

My work there was practically over, as the few patients who were left could be supplied from the regular mess hall, so I returned to my home in Brooklyn.

Some days later I crossed Fulton Ferry and, to my surprise, found Broadway deserted. The draft riot was spreading. From the 13th to the 16th of July, 1863, the streets were practically given over to a crowd of hoodlum boys brandishing clubs and sticks, rushing wildly and howling "Niggers, niggers! Hang the niggers!" They did hang some to lamp posts. Negro shanties were fired and occupants driven into the flames. A colored orphan asylum was attacked and burned. One poor fellow was chased for miles, and at last he jumped into a pool of water, preferring to drown rather than to be hanged or beaten to death. This riot, the most disgraceful and cowardly of all horrible crimes that ever disgraced modern New York City, resulted in the death of nearly one thousand people, mostly negroes, and was incited by two copperheads whose names should be abhorred forever.

A handsome boy patient of about seventeen years attached himself to me, much to my annoyance, and I found it difficult to give him the attention he desired. At last, however, to my great relief, he was ordered to report to his regiment, whence he wrote frequently. About six months later, to my astonishment, he came to my home, saying, "I was so homesick I just had to come, and I ran away without asking for a furlough." Of course he was liable to arrest as a deserter, and it cost me much persuasion and insistence at military headquarters, to convince them that the boy was ignorant of the treachery of his act. But finally, after much advice, he started for his regiment with a return pass. About a year later he wrote asking my advice as to his marrying "a very nice girl," as he thought "an economical wife could help him to save money,"—on twelve dollars a month, forsooth!

CHAPTER IV
The Great Manhattan Fair of the U. S. Sanitary Commission, 1864

"Yet Thou wilt hear the prayer we speak,
The song of praise we sing—
My children, who Thine Altar seek
Their grateful gifts to bring.

*   *   *   *   *

"Lo! for our wounded brothers' need,
We bear the wine and oil;
For us they faint, for us they bleed,
For them our gracious toil!"

OLIVER WENDELL HOLMES

While the devastations of Civil War were sending thousands of our brave men to die, and to sleep in distant graves, inadequate relief for sick and wounded soldiers also caused much unnecessary suffering and loss of life. Lacking more prompt means of assistance, supplies, surgeons, nurses, et cetera, could reach them only through the slow process of military regulations.

With the hope of supplying this most urgent need, the great Manhattan fair of the United States Sanitary Commission was suggested, and later organized by the efforts of the Rev. Doctor Bellows of New York City. He became its president, and, with other gentlemen as a committee, went to Washington to consult military and hospital departments as to some feasible manner of supplementing this most necessary branch of the United States service.

The congregation of All Souls' Church, of which Dr. Bellows was pastor, at once voted that the $40,000 that had been appropriated for a church steeple should be donated to the great Fair. The steepleless church stands to-day, a monument to their practical benevolence.

Their beneficent intention resulted in the erection of an immense wooden building at Union Square and Fourteenth Street, New York City, for a great bazaar. The opening took place on April 14th, 1864, the Honorable Joseph Choate delivering an address. An original poem by Oliver Wendell Holmes was sung by a union of many volunteer church choirs, before a vast multitude. The verses at the head of this chapter are selected from the poem.

The building was practically overflowing with the number of enormous donations that had no precedent, nor has any later benevolence in our country ever equalled this cheerful, spontaneous outpouring of money and salable goods, from all classes and individuals, merchants and dealers of every grade. These gifts of every description were piled high on shelves and in beautifully arranged booths, where charming young girls and earnest bright-eyed women competed in the selling of them to hundreds of eager buyers. Wealthy, generous patrons vied with one another in liberal purchases and donations, while those of smaller means were also happy in giving their mites to swell the enormous sums that astonished even the sanguine organizers. Many others, having no means to spare, volunteered their entire time and services to any department needing them, however laborious or unpleasant. And here they worked cheerfully every day until midnight during the three weeks of the fair, unconscious of weariness. Probably in no other bazaar were there ever such tireless workers, generous donors, or enthusiastic buyers. The united beneficence, patriotism and good will of these people poured into the treasury of the Sanitary Commission the enormous amount of two million dollars. This great sum for those days enabled the Commission to perfect an organization unparalleled in scope and efficiency, with a corps of faithful, honorable workers.

Like the Red Cross, which came to us later from Switzerland, this commission was immune from attack after battles. Often following the army closely, its representatives were able to set up temporary hospitals more quickly and efficiently with their independent supplies, army wagons and even transportation for special duty, than could be done by the regular army routine. Later my opportunity for knowing their work for soldiers was unusual. Being the only person in the hospital camp in the field working independently, without pay for any service, and provided with a pass from United States Army's Headquarters, the commission claimed that I was entitled to my living and any supplies I might require for the sick.

The relation here of an instance of personal experience will give some idea of the capability and prompt action of the commission immediately after the close of the war, and at almost the last moment of its field work, at City Point, Virginia.

The armies of the James and Potomac were ordered to Washington as speedily as transportation would permit. They were to take part in the grand review and were to be mustered out of service. The sick were also carried to Washington hospitals as soon as they were able to sail on the transports now crowding the docks of City Point. The headquarters of the United States Armies in the field had some time previously been transferred to Washington, where, still later, I often saw General Grant, always silent and smoking, except when in the presence of ladies.

General Russell, with his colored troops, was left in command at City Point to finish up the Government work there. Surgeon Thomas Pooley, later a distinguished oculist, of New York City, had been left in charge of the almost abandoned field hospital. Barracks and tents were dismantled, canvas roofs were removed and "turned in" to the Government, leaving only stockade walls, much useless camp furniture, and debris of all sorts that it would have been unprofitable to ship north.

Into these roofless wards swarmed crowds of destitute "contrabands" from the surrounding country and from Petersburg, eight miles distant, and settled down like flocks of crows. They found many things that were treasures to them among the abandoned supplies and rations upon which they subsisted until the government could devise some plan to save these helpless wandering creatures from starvation.

SURGEON THOMAS POOLEY

The word contraband as applied to negroes was first used May 23d, 1861, by General Ben Butler, soon after taking command of Fortress Monroe, when three slaves escaped from work on a Confederate fort, near by, and came across the river in a boat asking protection. The owner sent for them by flag of truce. General Butler decided that tho not strictly legal that as a war measure he was justified as they were property to their owners and that with all other property used against the Union they were "contraband of war," and refused to give them up. The number of runaway slaves to the fort "increased to $60,000 worth of negroes," who were put to work for the Union army,—many of whom enlisted and served faithfully till the end of the war.

At that time I was the only white woman in camp, waiting for orders to report to the New York State agency in Washington. A kind motherly old colored "auntie" seemed to consider me merely a child, and constantly followed me about, watched over me, and became my general guardian. General Russell kept a guard of four colored soldiers, with stacked arms, night and day, about my quarters for my safety.

I was about to start for Washington when we were surprised by a belated regiment,—of the 6th corps, I think,— of sick men toiling wearily into the deserted hospital camp, now in confusion as if a raid had torn everything asunder. There was not a furnished bed or bunk for these poor sick discouraged men to lie upon, nor was there any food for their famished bodies as they dropped upon the bare ground exhausted, almost fainting.

I still had the use of an ambulance, and in this emergency hastily ordered the driver to take me to City Point, one-half mile distant, for help. Fortunately the Sanitary Commission barge, loaded with surplus supplies, had not started, but was just about to cut loose, when I informed them of the destitution and helplessness of the sick stranded soldiers.

Mr. J. Yates Peek, formerly of the 147th New York Infantry, at once reversed orders, unpacked supplies, and put his men to work. By night the barracks were covered with canvas roofs; comfortable beds were made of fresh hay, and the men were fed. The "contrabands" cheerfully assisted me in preparing food and caring for the famished men. I think Doctor Pooley was the only surgeon in camp. Contrabands helped, in their rude way, to nurse the helpless, and a little camp sprang up and remained until the men were able to travel and get transportation to Washington. There was probably no better work done by this great organization than that by the belated company of agents of the United States Commission in that emergency. Without their help and supplies these men must have suffered keenly, and perhaps have died before relief could have been sent back from Washington on an unprecedented requisition, and the necessary "red tape" regulations complied with.

J. YATES PEEK

Another personal experience comes to mind. Months after the war, at their New York City Headquarters, when all liabilities of the Sanitary Commission had been met and field work disbanded, there was still a considerable balance in the treasury. The money had been collected for a specific purpose, namely—for the benefit of sick soldiers. This need was now supplied by the Government in various hospitals and in temporary homes, but the surplus money could not legally or honorably be applied to any other benevolence.

Finally it was agreed that soldiers' families were the legitimate heirs to this soldiers' fund. Therefore Mrs. Baldwin, a woman of great tact and capability, with myself, was asked to visit their families and judiciously assist the needy. Through that unusual bitterly cold winter of '65 and '66 we visited and assisted many of them. With the advent of warm weather the last dollar was expended, and the official life of this great beneficent work ended. Through it thousands of lives were saved, and many cheered and made comfortable.

At the Brooklyn Sanitary Fair over $400,000 were raised, and in Chicago and the West, that had led in this great movement, chiefly through the efforts of women, the amounts were astonishing. Through the great heart of the people, from all sources over $25,000,000 came into the treasury of the Sanitary Commission.

CHAPTER V
New England Rooms

Colonel Frank Howe, of the New England Rooms, on Broadway near Fulton Street, New York City, was the director of that Rest for stranded and sick soldiers, as well as for many helplessly wounded. Here I found many of the most interesting cases of my experience. Colonel Howe felt that their contribution of wounded to the Sanitary Fair would be a more effective object-lesson and incentive, than inanimate war emblems and relics displayed in the Arms and Trophy Department. Some of these crippled men were now waiting for Government to provide homes for those incapable of self-support.

Colonel Howe thereupon secured free passes for a number of convalescents, and I consented to take charge of them during the fair. Consequently, one bright day, the New England ambulance was crowded with the following passengers, namely: one man without legs, two men without arms, one blind from a shot passing through his head, a one-legged boy, the famous John Burns of Gettysburg, and a colored woman to assist. I sat on the front seat with the driver. We drove up Broadway to the fair grounds, quite regardless of the curious crowd that followed.

These brave martyrs were received with outstretched hands and cordial sympathy, and given the freedom of every department in the wonderful exhibition. In a splendid restaurant I volunteered to act as waiter, that I might be certain that the Boys had good meals and attention, for which the Sanitary Commission made no charge.

A crowd followed armless Berry who carried on his strong back legless Smith,—who in turn dressed and fed Berry. These two had become great friends and, like the

Siamese twins, were inseparable. Always cheerful, they seemed to enjoy life. Smith was a good penman and wrote me interesting letters, of which I still have some, generally signed "Berry and Smith." Berry often carried the legless man about the large building to see the wonders which they greatly enjoyed.

MCNULTY

Another armless soldier, a sergeant always in uniform, travelled about alone, and when in cars or boats was rarely asked for fare, or if so, he would say: "Help yourself from my pockets." Few had the heart to do this, so he usually travelled free.

McNulty, a refined young man, who had lost an arm in an early engagement, but was now quite well, was also of our party, though he was quite independent and asked no help, having already learned, like General Howard, to use his left arm for writing and to serve double duty.

Famous John Burns was included with those mentioned above in the freedom of the whole building, and at seventy years of age called himself one of my "Boys." The following is copied from a card which he had printed to "save so much talk," and which he claimed was a true history of his experience and help in the renowned battle of Gettysburg. This card he gave me personally.

JOHN L. BURNS' ACCOUNT OF HIMSELF

"I was born in Burlington, New Jersey, on the 5th day of September, 1793. I served in the war of 1812. At the outbreak of the Rebellion, I went with Captain McPherson to Camp Wayne, Westchester, where I enlisted, but was discharged at the end of a fortnight on account of my age. I returned to Gettysburg (my home at that time), then went to Hagerstown and served as assistant in the wagon camp for two weeks, after which, as a teamster, I joined the three months' boys under Patterson, with whom I remained a month. I then went to Frederick, and obtained the position of police officer in General Banks' division. I was present at the battle of Edward's Ferry, and saw Colonel Baker carried across the river. I remained with Colonel Banks for six months, and then returned home, where I was at the time of the battle of Gettysburg. On the first day of the fight I met General Reynolds, who had been out reconnoitering, and was asked to show him the Emmettsburg road. After doing this, I obtained a musket from a soldier who had been wounded while on guard, and went off to the army 'to shoot some of the damned rebels'. I fell in with a Wisconsin regiment, and fought sometimes in line, and sometimes on my own hook. About one P. M., during an intermission, while lying in the woods, I saw a Missouri man fall from the shot of a rebel concealed in the bushes. I stepped behind a tree, and seeing the rebel about to reload, I shot him. I also shot a tremendous great rebel who would not get out of my way. I myself received seven balls on the first day of the fight, the last of which wounded me severely in the leg. I lay on the field all night, and a rebel surgeon gave me water and a blanket. In the morning I crawled to a house near by, and about two P. M. succeeded in being taken to my own house, which I found occupied by the rebels as a hospital. Their doctor dressed my wound. On Friday, at two P. M. I was closely questioned by two rebel officers as to where I got my musket."

I have also his photograph which he gave me, and from which, I believe, the life size figure of his statue was made. I saw him many times at my home in Brooklyn, and elsewhere, always wearing proudly the shabby old coat with bullet holes in the front corners. This is not given in the life size figure of the old hero on his monument at Gettysburg Cemetery, where he stands without a coat with bared head, musket in hand, as if starting for the field of action.

"And as they gazed, there crept an awe
Through the ranks in whispers, and some men saw,
In the antique garments and long white hair,
The past of the nation, in battle there."

JOHN BURNS

CHAPTER VI
Arms and Trophy Department of the Sanitary Commission Fair

This department was beautifully draped with bunting, Revolutionary, Mexican and other old war flags, and also a few Confederate flags, captured by regiments, still in the field, that had yet many a bloody battle to fight. A number of distinguished, elegantly-gowned women toiled here indefatigably, brimming over with excitement and patriotism, quite regardless of the unusual fatigue of standing and working so many hours daily, in their anxiety to allow no one to pass without contributing in some way to the fund, now reaching thousands of dollars.

Here was to be decided the "sword test," that would indicate the most popular general, by the number of votes cast at one dollar each. The sword was to be presented to the winner of the largest number of votes. How these attractive ladies worked for their favorites! A magnetic thrill pervaded this room, where men of fashion and reputation crowded, ostensibly to learn how the vote was going.

Mrs. Grant, a noble-looking woman, accepted graciously, but without solicitation, all who offered votes for General Grant, of whom she invariably spoke as "Mr. Grant." Mrs. McClellan, with elegant society manner, lost no opportunity in gaining a vote for General McClellan; her vivacity, personal charm, and courteous flattery won many a vote for her husband. I think if her son, our ex-mayor, could have seen his mother at the height of her matured beauty he would have been justly proud.

The polls were to close at midnight on the last day of the fair. Excitement ran high as the hour approached. At ten minutes before the hour the McClellan vote was far ahead, and that party was already exulting, confident of success; but at five minutes before the final closing of the polls, the Union League, of Philadelphia, telegraphed, ordering "five hundred votes for Grant," and the sword was his.

MAJOR-GENERAL AND MRS. GEORGE B. MCCLELLAN

UNION LEAGUE HOUSE

Indignant Democrats pronounced this an act of treachery; an ominous dissent spread over the restless crowd, and for a time it seemed as if there might be some dangerous demonstration. Only the general refinement and restraint of the surging, self-respecting crowd prevented an outbreak.

Mrs. McClellan was pitifully disappointed, as her vision of the White House grew dim; and after the popular election of Grant, and the defeat of McClellan, she indignantly declared that she would not live in such an ungrateful country. She actually lived abroad for some years but, like all good Americans, she was happy to return to enjoy the freedom of her own native land.

In the month of February, 1909, I had the pleasure of seeing again, in the Smithsonian Museum at Washington, the veritable sword of that memorable contest, which had been presented in April, 1863. Other swords and equipments of General Grant were preserved in a large glass case. A silver head of Liberty formed the handle, set with diamonds, garnets and turquoises, the hilt and shield in bas-relief of a helmeted knight, the blade and scabbard highly wrought in oxidized silver and gold. The Chattanooga is the largest and finest of six or eight swords, all highly wrought and jeweled, which were presented by admiring friends at different dates to General Grant.

At the beginning of the Fair I had obtained permission for the three men, Smith, Berry and Mudge, to remain in the trophy department, where, each day, many greenbacks were crowded into their pockets. I had asked Mesdames Grant and McClellan to head subscription lists and to solicit money for the three helpless soldiers. Both ladies cheerfully and effectively urged people to subscribe at one dollar each, and at the close of the last evening they were happy to hand over to me, to be divided among these living martyrs of our cruel war, the sum of about five hundred dollars.

A citizen, employed by the New England Rooms, had charge of the finances and of the safe. He came every night with the ambulance to take me and the mutilated men back to the New England Rooms to sleep. On this last night I handed him the great roll of five hundred one-dollar bills to carry home and put into the safe. Instantly, however, an impulse came to me, and I said: "Just let me look at that money to see if it is all right." Grasping it firmly, I did not return it to the man, but carried it safely to the Rest, and kept it during the night. Before morning the scamp had robbed the safe and vanished, and of course was never more heard of. Was it telepathy or a finer psychic perception that saved the boys their money?

A unique incident occurred at this Rest, to the great amusement of the Boys. I frequently stayed here all night with the capable matron, Mrs. Russell, in her apartments on the top floor of this former store-house. One evening we were startled by unusual hilarity among the patients on the floor below. A great "well" was open through the middle of the building for the purpose of raising merchandise to the upper floors, and now it served as a fine ventilator. On stepping forward to the railing we saw to our astonishment three boys, each having lost a leg. They were great chums, always together, and sometimes the group was called "Three Legs." Each was on a crutch, carrying in one hand an artificial government leg, and they were having a grotesque dance with these limbs and crutches. To the men it seemed very funny and caused roars of laughter, but I failed to find amusement in the gruesome antics of these boys, scarcely of age, crippled for life.

"THREE LEGS"

Colonel Mrs. Daily, whom I met at the New England Rooms, enjoyed the unique honor of having been appointed adjutant on the staff of Governor Sprague, of Rhode Island. Colonel Daily had just returned from a tour of inspection of Rhode Island regiments stationed near the front and had also visited sick soldiers in different hospitals. She had prepared and published a general and statistical report of the condition of the men to present officially to Governor Sprague.

COLONEL MRS. DAILY

After my success in collecting funds for Mudge, Smith and Berry at the Sanitary Fair, I concluded to take them to the great exposition then being held at Philadelphia, but for some unexplained reason my efforts to secure financial aid for them met with comparative failure.

A handsome ambulance of the Wicacoe fire engine company had met us at Camden boat landing, Philadelphia, whence we were driven to the famous Union Volunteer Refreshment Saloon and Hospital, where a few cots for special cases had been set up in the private offices. Here these three men were warmly welcomed and made comfortable during their visit.

Mrs. Lincoln called there one day, and, after a pleasant talk, gave twenty dollars to each of the "Twins." They seemed to appreciate her kindly words even more than her practical gift.

When troops were approaching the city of Philadelphia, the great "Liberty Bell" rang out a welcome to coming regiments. Hundreds of kindly women, laden with good things, hastened to this large building, which was a cooper's shop, quickly set up rough tables, and spread their generous supplies ready for the hungry men. During the war thousands of men and many regiments halted here for "a good square meal," while passing through the city to the front. When the hungry Boys were rested and satisfied, they fell into line and marched away to the music of the jolly fife and drum, cheering and shouting their thanks, only exceeded in sound by the deafening applause of the patriotic people waiting to see them off. This "shop," by the generosity of its owners, and the unflagging patriotism of the women, became historical. Many full regiments remembered the good things freely given by those who had not always an abundant living for themselves.

The following is a verbatim copy of a letter written by one of the "Twins" from the Union Volunteer Refreshment Saloon and Hospital, generally known as the Cooper Rest Hall, referred to above:

> "Philadelphia, June 22d, 1864.
> Miss Adelaide Smith:

Dear Madam:—
I have just received your kind and welcome letter and now hasten to reply. I am glad to hear of your safe arrival in New York, and regret that friend Mudge cannot exercise sufficient control over himself to prevent so much useless trouble to his friends but I anticipated as much. I hope the air of the Astor House will be congenial to him. Berry has been seeking the paper you refer to but has not yet gotten it. He will go out to-day and get it, if he can, and send it to you.

Shortly after Berry went out with you, the day you left, Mrs. Lincoln visited the Saloon and had a little talk with me (Smith) and a $20.00 bill was slipped into my hand. I believe there is $20.00 expected for Berry from the same source.

With regard to pecuniary matters Philadelphia is looking up. In addition to the above donation I have received $25.00, and Berry about $20.00. Berry is out occasionally, hence the difference between us, but Berry will stay in the Saloon alongside of me and no doubt we will both share alike.

Berry was walking along Chestnut Street on Monday when a man standing at a doorway stopped him, questioned him, did he know Miss Furness? Yes. Well Miss Furness has been everywhere trying to find us, wishing very much to see us. Miss Furness was then in the house. Berry was invited in to see her. She commenced the old story about the artificial arms and legs. We expect she will go to the fair and peddle out the rest of her old jewelry which will, she expects, enable her to give us some fifteen or twenty thousand dollars each. In fact our expectations are raised to such a pitch and we are so sanguine of Miss Furness that we shall probably have a surplus of a few thousand, dear Madam for you, as a 'slight testimonial of our esteem and mark of our gratitude'; etc., etc. She has also a box full of artificial arms and legs.

Will you please tell Price to forward all letters there may be in the hospital for Berry and me. Mr. Redner has not yet called.

I hope Mr. D. will get my furlough extended, at any rate I shall stay here some time longer. We are getting along very comfortably. There is nothing particular in the way of news. Berry and I went out sailing a day or two ago.

All the good folks here beg to be remembered to you, Mr. Wade in particular. Our best regards to all our friends, Mr. D. especially, and believe us, dear Madam,

Yours very gratefully,
Albert A. Smith and John H. Berry

P. S. If you have time, in case you pass through Philadelphia, to call and see us, it will afford us much pleasure."

On our return to New York, as in going to Philadelphia, every one wished to lend a helping hand, but Smith clung to Berry, who carried him with ease, while the crowd cheered the courageous, independent fellows. On returning them safely to the New England Rooms, I longed to rest for a few days at my home in Bedford Avenue, Brooklyn, but I found at the Rooms a slowly dying woman who greatly excited my sympathy. She had been brought from Washington, where she had contracted dysentery while nursing her son, who died soon after she reached him. She was on her way to her home in Worcester, Massachusetts. There was no proper place for the poor soul, and Colonel Howe was anxious to have her reach her home before she died, so I took charge of her, and we went by the Fall River Line. I sat beside her stretcher all night in the ladies' cabin, watching her pulse and constantly giving her stimulants or nourishment. At daybreak we reached Worcester. The man sent to assist me found an express wagon on which the stretcher was placed, and we all drove to a plain comfortable-looking house. Finding no responsible person about the place I took possession of the parlor on the second floor, ordering a bed from another room. The feeble woman was then carried up and placed comfortably at rest in her own home. The doctor came and, against my earnest protest, insisted on stopping the stimulants at once, saying he knew her constitution better than I. When her husband appeared he showed no particular interest save to take possession of her pocketbook, and I did not see him again.

A Mr. and Mrs. Green showed much interest for the woman. They kindly took me to their home for rest. Later in the day I went back to see the fast failing woman, who died two days later, a victim to the conceit of an ignorant doctor. I enjoyed for a day or two the hospitality of the Greens, and I shall never forget their home-grown strawberries and cream.

CHAPTER VII
The Unique Case of William Mudge of Lynn, Massachusetts

This narrow-breasted, delicate boy of about twenty-one years, enlisted in the Thirty-third Massachusetts Infantry, and, with his regiment, went into the battle of Chancellorsville on Sunday morning, May 2d, 1863. After once regaining the field they were defeated with considerable loss in prisoners and many wounded. Mudge fell by a shot passing entirely through his head, cutting both optic nerves. A friend in the regiment from his city, tied a handkerchief about his head and left him to die, then ran to join his regiment, fearing capture by the enemy. As soon as a chance offered he wrote to Mudge's father, who was president of a Lynn bank, telling him that his son had been left dying on the battlefield.

Mr. Mudge started at once to find the dead body of his son, and succeeded in reaching the Confederate lines, where they began to search for the body, which could not be found on the battlefield. The boy was at last discovered alive, lying neglected in the Confederate field hospital.

It was often impossible for the surgeons and detailed nurses to care for all the wounded, and so they gave their time to those having a chance of living, which poor Mudge certainly did not seem to have. The gunshot wound had caused his face to turn quite black, so that his father, in hunting among the hopelessly wounded, did not recognize him; but the boy knew his father's voice and called out, and so was rescued from a slow death. Mudge told his story to me essentially as follows:

WILLIAM MUDGE

"I lay all night on the field, drenched by a shower (which often happens after a battle). In the morning Confederate soldiers were detailed to bury the dead, and were preparing to carry me to the open trench near by. When I spoke to them feebly they gave me water from a canteen, and left me, feeling sure I would die before morning. Imagine what a night that must have been! The brushwood near where I was lying took fire, and I narrowly escaped being burned to death. When the men came on the third day to bury the dead, I had become so weak I could only move my little finger to show life. The Johnnies then said—'This fellow is good stuff, let's take him in.'"

It was easy for the father to get permission to take away this apparently dying prisoner. Going by easy stages to Washington, it was found on examination that the boy was permanently blind and had lost an eye. His skull was said to have been fractured so that there were not two inches of solid cranium, the jaw bones and teeth were destroyed.

Surgeons with much skill trepanned a hole in the skull with a silver plate, and with the assistance of skilled dentists, they manufactured jaw bones and teeth. They had fitted him with a glass eye, and green glasses to cover the defects, so that some months after, when I met him at the New England Rooms, he had the appearance of a well-dressed, refined, though rather frail blind man.

During the fair I had taken care of him and walked him about the great halls explaining many things that he could not, of course, see or understand, and he came to consider my opinions final. He carried to his home in Lynn about three hundred dollars from the fair subscription and other benevolent sources.

A few weeks later his mother wrote me, saying that William had become so unhappy and irritable that they could not manage him, and he had so often said that if Miss Smith were there, she would know what would make him more contented. Mrs. Mudge begged me to come, if only for a short visit. This I could not well refuse; and I found a pleasant refined family in a comfortable home of their own. Mr. Mudge, William's father, was a gentleman and a bank president. I will digress here for a few words on an observation, quite surprising to me. Early on Sunday morning I saw Mr. Mudge and several other gentlemen coming up the street, each carrying a newspaper and two large bundles. This seemed quite strange, but was explained at breakfast by the inevitable down-east baked beans in a crock, and a loaf of hot brown bread which had been at the bake shop all night. It was the custom for gentlemen to bring them home on Sunday morning. Certainly they were delicious. Being of New York blood, I was not "au fait" on the customs regarding baked beans and brown bread.

William's mother told me that he was almost transformed when under my influence. His was a restless nervous temperament, and this, added to his blindness, made life miserable. His fastidious tastes and conventionality continued. One Sunday, in church, he whispered, "Is my back hair parted straight?"—this being the style for men at that time. And again, "Am I holding my prayer-book right side up?" He needed occupation; but what could the blind boy do?

Accidentally I saw in a newspaper an advertisement for young men to sell a book of the early history of the war, and I proposed to Mudge that he could sell this book. But his aristocratic ideas were hard to overcome, until I insinuated that he might have a valet to carry the books and take care of him. This modified his ideas on my suggestion.

His memory of locality was surprising. When he escorted me to Boston "to see the town" he would say, "Now over there is the bird-cage (a shop) and there is the flat-iron sign, so we must go this way." Only once he failed, and then he said we must go back to the bird-cage, after which we started again all right.

I went with him to Boston, and had an interview with the agent, who was greatly pleased to have a martyr of the war to sell the book. I imperatively urged Mudge to start at once, which he did with his valet the next day; when I also left Lynn. He wrote from memory in a good clear hand, with a little slat to guide his pen, of his phenomenal success, which was such as we expected. During his tour about Massachusetts he called at the home of the poet Longfellow, who sent me a much prized photograph with his autograph.

Many bought of the poor boy, out of sympathy and patriotism, this very imperfect book, which, doubtless, they never read. In the course of a year he again wrote that he had opened a stationery store in Lynn, and was doing a good business; and later he employed four clerks. Still later I was dumbfounded on receiving an announcement of his marriage.

HENRY WADSWORTH LONGFELLOW

Three years after, when I visited their pretty cottage on Lynn Beach, near that of Fanny Davenport the actress, William was not at home, but I saw his charming wife and their handsome, healthy boy of sixteen months.

CHAPTER VIII
The Start for the Front

"Woman should take to her soul a strong purpose, and then make circumstances conform to that purpose."

SUSAN B. ANTHONY

My work for sick soldiers began early in 1862, in the "Department of the East," which included Long Island Hospital, Willett's Point, David's Island, Fort Schuyler and Bedloe's Island (now Liberty); all of these hospitals being in charge of Surgeon McDougall.

This extensive experience prepared me for work at the front, which, after many futile efforts, I could now reach through a society known as "Masonic Mission," by which a pass was secured from General Ben Butler for myself and three assistant nurses, and which gave me the anxiously desired privilege and authority of going to the "front," with these nurses, who were quite unknown to me.

We sailed July 24th, 1864, on the Patapsco, a government transport that had carried sick soldiers to New York, and was returning to City Point for orders, and were the only passengers on board.

Fatigue and the odor of bilge water induced intense "mal de mer," which, added to insubordination on the part of two of my assistants, caused the usual distress and despair.

The atmosphere of my state room was intolerable, and the captain kindly ordered a mattress placed on deck for me, where I was comparatively comfortable until I was obliged to stagger below on hearing of unseemly conduct on the part of the two nurses. I threatened, with good effect, to have the captain put them ashore at the first island we came to. Fortunately they did not know that we would sight no island on that short voyage. The third assistant, good Mrs. Dunbar, in her kindly, motherly way, was my only comfort.

The captain had tried, in vain, to arouse me by an alarm that the Alabama was chasing us. But sea-sickness knows not even the law of self-preservation, and I replied, "I'd as lief as not go down by the Alabama or in any other way."

At night I refused to go below to my stateroom and bilge water odor, quite regardless of the captain's perplexity. After some hesitancy, however, he gave me the only stateroom on deck. This was filled with the accoutrements of a Confederate officer whom, as a prisoner of war, the captain had just delivered over to the government prison at Fort Lafayette, in the narrows of New York Bay. I awoke at night in such perfect peace and comfort that for a time I imagined the Alabama had really run us down, and that I was now happy in heaven.

My stateroom door had been left open for air, and, stepping out on deck, I found there was no motion or sound, save a soft ripple of water against the bow. A full perfect moon cast a broad silvery path across the quiet waters, so intense that it seemed quite possible that Jesus had indeed walked upon the Sea of Galilee. There was no one in sight, nor was there a sound of anything living or moving, though the "watch" probably saw me leaning over the railing. We had anchored at the mouth of the James River, waiting for the pilot.

On the morning of July 29th, we again anchored, this time before City Point, Virginia, at the junction of the James and Appomatox Rivers, headquarters of the United States armies in the field under command of General Grant.

I went ashore in a little boat with the captain, and reported to the Provost Marshall at headquarters, to show my pass from General Butler. The camp appeared rather shabby. There were only a few wooden buildings, used by army officers, a number of large tents and negro cabins, with guards and officers running from one tent to another. City Point was a barren, almost treeless country of untilled land. The United States flag floated over a small house used by General Grant as headquarters.

A small narrow, cigar-shaped, back-wheel boat, the "Gazelle," returned with me to the "Patapsco," and taking on board the three nurses we steamed up the narrow Appomatox River, a monotonous sail of six miles between low bluffs and sparse foliage, to the hospital tents at Point of Rocks, which were pitched on the very brink of this malarious stream. This was General Butler's Hospital Department of the James.

For the first time I realized my strange position, and felt, when the "Patapsco" was out of sight, as if "I had burned my bridges behind me." There were only half a dozen men and officers aboard. Feeling impelled to speak to a refined-looking man, wearing major's shoulder-straps, I found him very courteous. I remarked on my apprehension of the strangeness of the situation, and said if I could feel assured that the surgeon in charge of Point of Rocks Hospital was a gentleman, I should have nothing to fear. I asked the Major if he knew that officer; he replied that he did, and thought I would find him a gentleman.

On reaching Point of Rocks Hospital, the Major offered to go ashore and send an ambulance for us, and this took us a short distance to the hospital tent wards, and to a small frame house near to the Hospital Headquarters.

I called a passing orderly and reported at once with my Butler pass, to the officer in charge, and found, to my consternation, while the color rose to the roots of my hair, that this man was the very Major to whom I had spoken on the boat. Rising and bowing politely he said, "Miss Smith, I trust you will always find me a gentleman."

It was well for me that he was a gentleman, for I found myself in a very anomalous position, having been sent by the Masonic Mission to take the place of Clara Barton, who was already in charge of this work, but away at the time. I soon discovered that the Masonic Mission had taken advantage of Miss Barton's absence and—quite without authority—had sent me to take her place. The Major, Surgeon Porter, however, courteously invited me to remain until her return.

Meanwhile he had ordered a large tent put up for my assistants and, as a compliment, assigned me to a room at headquarters. But sleeping with a strange fat woman on a feather-bed, with windows closed on a hot July night was too much honor; so the next morning I asked to be allowed to go with the nurses in their large new tent, where, with a cot in each corner, we were quite comfortable. A small tent was attached for my mess-room, while the nurses ate at the "patients' mess."

General Butler's army headquarters of the Department of the James, was across the Appomattox, at Bermuda Hundreds, whence the rumbling of wagons and tramping of troops over pontoon bridges could be heard through the silence and darkness of the night. Of course I slept little on my first night in camp.

The next night I was greatly distressed by groans and cries in the distance and, much excited, I went directly to Surgeon Porter, as early as allowable the next morning, to ask if I could do something for the suffering soldiers. Seeming surprised at my question he replied that he was not aware of such suffering in camp. He asked where the sounds came from, and as I indicated the direction he said with a curious expression: "Well, Miss Smith, you may try if you wish, but the cries come from the mules in the corral, and I fear you will not succeed." That joke followed me wherever I went.

Surgeon Porter gave me charge of the officers' ward, of perhaps forty or more patients. Each officer having his own orderly in attendance, and the hospital being in very good running order, there was no unpleasant work for me to do. So at first I saw only the romantic side of "bathing feverish brows," and giving comforting words, with some specially prepared diet.

Not caring for society, or mere sentiment, I soon resolved to ask for a ward of private soldiers, who did not presume upon equality, though many of them were as truly gentlemen as were their officers.

Meanwhile the three nurses, though untrained, like most nurses of that time, did good work in the wards of the regular soldiers.

CHAPTER IX
Some Patients

Point of Rocks Hospital consisted of about a dozen tents, each perhaps fifty feet long, pinned as usual to the ground with wooden pegs. These contained bunks and cots on either side, for about forty or more patients to each tent, and sometimes, when crowded, patients had only straw or hay bags with a blanket on the bare ground, all of which the men nurses were expected to keep in perfect order and cleanliness.

To enter at one end of these tents and see the rows of sick and suffering, despondent men, at once aroused an earnest desire to help them to a little comfort and cheer.

One day, passing through a long ward, I was startled by the sight of a little pinched face with great dark eyes, that looked as if its owner might be about ten or twelve years old. Stepping quickly to the cot I said, "Why, who are you, and where did you come from?"

A feeble voice replied, "I'm Willie, I was here yesterday when you passed, but you didn't look at me."

"But where did you come from?"

"I belong to the 37th New Jersey Infantry, in camp a few miles off, and I got sick and they brought me here."

"How could you be enlisted? How old are you?"

"I'm fifteen. I lied, and swore I was eighteen, and my parents wouldn't let me go, so I ran away, an'—an' I guess, I'll never see mother any more."

The soldier nurse said he was a typhoid case, with a chance of living, if he could have good care, but that he would not be persuaded to eat. I returned to him at once, saying, "Willie, I hear that you don't eat anything."

"I can't eat."

"O, but you must. Now, Willie, can't you think of

something you'd like?"

"Well," with a suppressed sob, "if I could get anything like mother used to make, perhaps I could."

"Now tell me, Willie, what it was, what did it look like, and how did it taste?"

The sick boy's description was not very clear, but I said cheerfully, "O, I can make that," and ran off to my tent and soon prepared something which, with a silver cup, spoon, and a tidy serviette, at least looked inviting in contrast with the battered tin cups and plates of camp life. He showed some interest as I said, "Here, Willie, is just what mother used to make." And he took a few spoonfuls quite cheerfully as I fed him. I asked if it did not taste something like mother made. He thought it did.

Feeling sure that only the greatest care would save him, I went at once to Surgeon Porter, saying, "Doctor, I'd like to have that boy, Willie, for an orderly."

"What, another?" he replied, laughing. "You have more orderlies now than General Grant himself."

"This is true, doctor," I said, for I had four who had been assigned to me by the doctor that they might have special care, "and not one of them can stand alone for one hour."

"Well, you may have him, and I wish you success."

I then asked Willie if he would like to be my orderly, and he seemed quite delighted. I directed the nurse to dress him early next morning, and to let him lie down till I came for him. The poor boy staggered to his feet, but we almost carried him to my tent, where I removed his army shoes and put a pair of my slippers on his poor, little thin feet. I then laid him on my cot, bathed his hot head, neck and hands, gave him nourishment, and told him to try to sleep while I was away caring for other patients. All this was repeated for several days, and thus he escaped the sight of dying and suffering men. Each night I took him back to his tent, where he slept soundly until morning. He improved slowly.

One day, while taking my dinner alone in my little mess tent, I was surprised to see him standing at "attention" beside me. "Miss Smith," he said, while the fever burned his cheeks and brightened his dark eyes, "I've been here five days, and it's time I did something for you." The fever had burned out for the time, and, turning quickly I caught his falling, emaciated form. Realizing his own helplessness, the poor child wept bitterly.

Meanwhile his youthful officers had come to see him, which greatly pleased the poor boy. He improved very slowly, but evidently would not quite recover in these surroundings. I decided to make an effort to send him home as soon as possible. With permission of Surgeon Porter, and with his ambulance and an orderly, I rode a few miles to a camp of the 37th New Jersey Infantry, in the woods, which was composed entirely of boys and officers of not more than twenty or twenty-four years of age.

The little "dog" or A tents allowed only one to crawl in on either side of the tent pole, and lie on his blankets on the bare ground with knapsacks for pillows. No wonder malaria made havoc in their ranks!

While I was there, an order came to send forward a small detachment of men for picket duty. All clamored to go, shouting in a most informal manner, quite regardless of discipline. "Say, Cap, let me go." "I say, Maj, you know me." "Cap, let me go, won't you?" etc., etc. A dozen men were selected, not one fully grown, and these boys staggered off in high spirits, each carrying a knapsack weighing sixty pounds, a gun and an overcoat.

The colonel and captain of this regiment very cheerfully made the necessary application for a sick furlough, and on my return to camp Surgeon Porter at once endorsed it. Then, having waited a few days for some one to take charge of Willie, I had the satisfaction of seeing him start in an ambulance for the boat at City Point, supplied with brandy and nourishment. His head lay on the knee of an officer who was going to Fortress Monroe, and there was a happy boyish smile on his face as they drove away.

In a few weeks came the good news that he had reached home and mother and was fast recovering.

In the same ward with Willie were a number of Ohio "ninety days selected men," chiefly farmers, nearly every man six feet or more in height. They were typhoid cases, who were really suffering more from nostalgia than from fever. They had already served half their term, yet nothing could arouse them from despair and homesickness, from which many of them actually died, while the wiry, irrepressible city boys generally recovered.

One day, while I was trying to bathe away the fever from the head and hands of a young officer, General Butler entered the tent with some of his staff, and thanked me for my care of this favorite, asking that I would do all in my power to make him comfortable.

Another patient, Chaplain Eaton, of a Connecticut regiment, was recovering from typhoid, and, though not very ill at this time, still claimed a good deal of my attention. I felt, however, that it was a waste of time to spend many minutes talking with him, or in reading the Bible to him, while so many others were really suffering and needing special care. But I wrote to his wife and did what I could. He was very grateful, and wished to prove it by presenting to me a handsome black horse, that his orderly brought daily to the tent for inspection and petting. The animal was so intelligent that he seemed really to recognize me. The chaplain's insistence upon my accepting the horse was quite annoying; and at last I said to him that "it would be a great pity to turn such a beautiful creature into an 'elephant', which he would certainly become on my hands."

CHAPTER X
Experiences at Point of Rocks

On Miss Barton's return I found myself very much "de trop," though she treated me kindly. I saw very little of her work, but her extreme deliberation, when one day I had run to her quite breathless from the operating tent for bandages, etc., for the surgeons who were waiting, was very irritating. She asked about my health, urged me to take a seat, and very slowly rummaged about for the necessary supplies. The only time I saw her actively engaged was on a day when there had been a skirmish at the front, and she started for the field with the ambulance and an orderly, and a small box of bandages, condensed milk, etc.

One bright moonlight night, I was startled by strange sounds of melodious singing in the distance, and, with an orderly, I went to ascertain its meaning. We soon came upon a large fire surrounded by a circle of perhaps forty negroes, men and women, crooning and singing. They were often led by a high falsetto, then sinking to a low monotone, when suddenly another voice would rise changing to a new refrain, while not one lost the time or pitch or made discords. They danced hand in hand in a slow rythmic circle, while one, more excited than the rest, would spring up to a remarkable height shouting, "Glory! bress de Lawd!" "I's a-comin' Lawd!" etc. All "eyes in a fine frenzy rolling," shone like great black beads in the firelight, while their white teeth gleamed brightly. All were in solemn seriousness as they sang simple couplets like the following:

"If I'd a died when I was young,
I wouldn't a had dis risk to run."
"Some folks is bery good on de sing,

But dey don't know nuffin 'bout de hebbenly King."
"Some folks is bery good on de talk,
But dey don't know nuffin 'bout de hebbenly walk."

They continued on in childish simplicity till their ecstasy broke into shouts of "Cum down Lawd!"—"I's a comin' Lawd! Look out for me!"—"I's a-waitin' Lawd!"—while the circle whirled in dizzy speed until they sometimes fell exhausted to the ground. All feared the "Voodou-Cunger" woman, and were anxious to propitiate her with a rabbit's foot and various incantations.

Eloquence, rhythm, oratory and harmony seem inborn among this strange people, who have given to the whole South the soft voice and accent so many of us like to hear.

Under existing conditions it was a relief when Mrs. E—— came from the Masonic Mission in New York and claimed that a mistake had been made in sending me to Point of Rocks, and informed me that I would find work to my liking at City Point.

The following day Mrs. E——, with an ambulance, took me for a day's rough travel over corduroy roads and ditches and through woods to General Burnside's 9th Corps headquarters in a clump of trees before Petersburg. The General came out of an inner tent, putting on his coat and apologizing, saying he had been sleeping.

"Why, General, how can you sleep with the shells screaming and exploding so near?"

"Oh," he replied, laughingly, "this is when I can sleep comfortably. It's only when I hear musketry that I fear there is mischief brewing."

A very courteous, handsome, soldierly gentleman was General Burnside.

We then drove a short distance to General O. B. Wilcox's headquarters, so near Petersburg that, with the General's glasses, I could distinctly see the people in their houses at their daily work, though the cannons on both sides were replying with a formality as if war was a matter of etiquette. There seemed to be only women in the town, going about their home duties, quite unconscious of shells falling into their doomed city. The General was quite elated at having that day moved his lines forward three-quarters of a mile.

Seeing a number of barrels piled before his tent, I asked why they were there. He smiled and said, "I was sitting here awhile ago when a bullet passed over my shoulder, and the boys were afraid a sharpshooter might pick me off, so they piled these barrels up for protection."

General Burnside commanded the 9th Army Corps and General Wilcox the second division of that Corps. Both were gentlemen of refinement and great kindness to the men, who were very proud and fond of their commanders. I observed that both Generals treated me with more courtesy than they showed to Mrs. E——, although she was a much older woman.

GENERAL BURNSIDE

The next day on leaving the hospital at Point of Rocks, after thanking Surgeon Porter for his friendliness and attention that had made my stay possible and pleasant, and bidding Miss Barton good-bye, I went with Mrs. E—— on board the "Gazelle," (then well known in New York Bay),—and returned to City Point.

We went directly to the tent of a Miss Nye, on the Agency Row, whom I recognized as having seen in the office of the Masonic Mission in New York City. Miss Nye at once took me aside saying, "You had better take off that badge,"—the badge of the Masonic Mission, which I had worn for protection,—"it is not respected here, and you may stay with me as long as you wish, but that woman cannot stay another night in my tent."

About midnight a terrific storm arose and threatened to sweep Miss Nye's tent into the ravine quite nearby. She called for help from the next tent, where slept some Christian Commission agents. While Miss Nye held on to one side of the tent, I threw myself across my cot and, with all my strength, held on to the other side. Mrs. E—— in a short gown and petticoat of the olden time, held the tent flaps as the wind rushed through, nearly carrying us all away with the tents. However, the men soon hammered down the tent pins securely, and all was quiet again. Altogether we made a comical picture and would have been a fine group for the present day kodak.

Mrs. E—— left City Point the next day, and so passed out of my life.

While I was yet with Miss Nye, another night of alarm ended rather amusingly. We were sleeping soundly on opposite sides of the tent when Miss Nye screamed out that some one had reached under the tent and touched her hand. We got up and, after talking loudly for a while, thought the intruder was scared off. Then we fell asleep. He came back again, however, evidently trying to reach a pocket book under Miss Nye's pillow. This time, not wishing to disturb the sleepers in the near tents, we concluded to "arm ourselves for the fray." Miss Nye found a hatchet which she would have used bravely. I could find no defensive weapon but a big long-necked bottle. We knew that the thief could hear our threatening talk as he was hiding in the ravine close by, so we lay down again, Miss Nye clasping the hatchet on her breast, and I embracing in like manner my big bottle. We soon slept soundly again, when suddenly a terrific crash caused us to spring up in alarm. What could it be? Then I realized that I had relaxed my hold on the big bottle, which had rolled across the rough floor and crashed against the tent pole. After indulging in a good laugh over our fright, we slept soundly once more until morning.

Still another incident regarding Miss Nye comes to mind. Years after the war I succeeded in finding her, then a graduate of homœopathy in New York City,—Doctor Frances M. Nye. She had met a Confederate soldier, also a graduate of this school of medicine, and also bearing the name of Francis M. Nye. The identity of names, perhaps, induced a lasting friendship, and when they married Miss Nye changed only one letter in her name. They continued to practise together for many years and seemed very happy.

CHAPTER XI
Depot Field Hospital and State Agencies at City Point, Virginia

The hospital was situated half a mile from General Grant's headquarters at City Point, at the junction of the James and Appomatox Rivers, and about eight miles from Petersburg front. The hospital camp, then under the charge of Surgeon Edward Dalton and medical staff, was laid out with great precision. This field hospital was divided into the 9th, 2d, 6th, 5th corps, and corps d'Afric, and these again into divisions, avenues, and streets at right angles,—numbered and lettered. There were many thousands of sick and wounded in these wards, nine thousand or more at a time, I believe.

Convalescent soldiers did police, ward, nurse and kitchen duty. There were hundreds of wards with stockade sides, covered with canvas roofs upheld in the usual manner by ridge and tent poles, each containing probably fifty or more bunks or cots. A perfect system of order and policing by convalescent men was enforced, and not a particle of refuse or any scrap was allowed to lie for a moment upon the immaculate streets or avenues of the "Sacred Soil," which was generally beaten hard and dry, though in wet weather this was a problem to try men's souls and women's soles too. At such times we were obliged to wade through nearly a foot of liquid mud, occasionally sticking fast till pulled out somehow, perhaps with the loss of a high rubber boot.

The wards were wonders of cleanliness, considering the disadvantages of field life, and even at that time sanitation was of a high order and, to a great degree, prevented local diseases. Men nurses, soldiers unfit for active duty, took pleasure in fixing up their wards with an attempt at ornamentation, when allowed. These men well deserved their pay, as they worked cheerfully for the government and for their sick comrades, doing their part faithfully during the devastations of war. They were as much needed and as necessary as their heroic comrades in the field. I never knew of one of these faithful, hard-working amateur nurses being guilty of neglect or unkindness, though chronic growlers and irritable sick men were often exasperating to the nurse's unfailing care and patience. They frequently conveyed some interdicted luxuries from the sutler, or extra rations, to make life more endurable and comfortable for the invalids. This was usually winked at by their officers. They were generally appreciated, and little dissatisfaction or complaint could have been expressed. Perfect discipline and sympathy seemed to prevail.

SANITARY COMMISSION TENT AT CITY POINT

During my year in this Field Hospital I did not hear of any enforcement of severe punishment, but I remember, one day, while riding outside of hospital lines, past a post or camp in the woods, seeing in the distance a poor fellow hanging by his thumbs to the branch of a tree. It was said by the men of his regiment that "the fellow ought to have been hanged."

Just across the road on one side of the hospital was a row of State Agency tents. Larger tents of the Sanitary Commission,—that magnanimous gift of the people that so often, even in the far South, so nobly supplemented the regular hospital work and supplies, sometimes even with its own transports and its own official corps of workers,—headed this row. In the middle of the Agency row were the tents of the Christian Commission, supported chiefly by churches from all over the Northern States. They had built a large rough wooden structure where regular services were held on Sundays and on many evenings during the week, to the great relief and enjoyment of weary men seeking to find a word of hope and comfort, and a change from the monotony of ward life. Many ministers and other speakers came to look over the work, and many of them were very interesting and earnest.

Along this extensive row of tents were the Agencies, supported by the liberality of their several States, which also supplemented the government in giving special care to their own individual men. Capable men and refined women workers toiled uncomplainingly to make hospital life more endurable for the sick.

From Petersburg front sick and wounded were daily sent to the hospital, often on rough flat sand cars, over badly laid shaking tracks, being brought as hastily as possible that they might receive proper care and help. The sight of these cars, loaded with sufferers as they lay piled like logs, waiting their turn to be carried to the wards,—powder-stained, dust-begrimed, in ragged torn and blood-stained uniforms, with here and there a half-severed limb dangling from a mutilated body,—was a gruesome, sickening one, never to be forgotten, and one which I tried not to see when unable to render assistance.

Not only were the sick and wounded from near by brought there, but large numbers came from more southerly points of the army of the Potomac. Many seriously or permanently injured were sent here to wait until able to be forwarded to Washington. Some came en route on sick furloughs, or to be discharged, or when fit returned to their regiments in the field. Every grade of suffering or weariness found temporary shelter and care here. All incurable cases were hurried forward as soon as possible to make room for the multitude still coming.

One day while I was passing through a large ward, a

number of sick and wounded men were brought in. Suddenly one of them,—a boy of about eighteen,—stood before me at "attention." Signs of typhoid were only too evident, as quite wildly, he struggled to express himself, much like the following:

JOHN C. GUFFIN

"Oh, Miss, won't you just take my name? It's John C. Guffin; and write to my parents and tell them about me?" Controlling himself with an effort he continued: "And Oh, do write to my employer, Mr. Gibson, in Albany, and now, now be quick, won't you?"—always prepared for such emergencies, I quickly took down these addresses,—"for in a minute I won't know anything, just like I was when they brought me in."

With a painful struggle he controlled his mind, saying: "Just take these" (small articles) "and this little watch and wear it until I get well." This intense strain exhausted the last gleam of intelligence, and he fell unconscious on a cot near by. Many weeks he lay, raving and incoherent, till the fever had spent its malign power. During these weeks I had many times stopped to glance at the poor fellow, with burning fever and his eyes rolling wildly; but I could do little for him. The soldier nurses, always kind to their sick comrades, did all that was necessary or possible.

At this crisis Dr. O'Maugher came to me in the Maine State Agency saying, "Do you remember the boy Guffin? Well the fever has spent itself, and he is now lying in a critical state of exhaustion, refusing all nourishment. I know you are over-worked, but he is at a point when only a woman's care can pull him through. Can you make a place for him on your list?"

I went as soon as possible to the emaciated patient, whose mind was not yet quite clear, though he seemed at once to have confidence in me and wished me to stay by his side. Losing no time, I said: "Why, John, I hear you will not eat anything, and now if you will not eat you will certainly relapse and die."

"I can't eat, I can't eat," he continued to repeat.

"Why not?" I asked. "Why can't you eat?"

"Why," he said, "these ain't John C. Guffin's teeth, and I can't eat, I can't eat."

Here was a problem. The boy must not be forced against his own will. "Why, my boy, that's nonsense, because you have had a bad fever."

He repeated, "Can't eat, can't eat; these ain't my teeth, and I can't eat with another man's teeth."

Experience had taught us many devices while in our daily care of irresponsible patients, so I replied quickly, "O, that makes no difference, don't you know you can eat just as well with another man's teeth as with your own?"—a fact painfully true to many. He turned and looked at me very doubtfully while I repeated and urged him to try. "Now, John, I'm going to make something real nice for you, and you are going to eat it."

Very soon I brought my little tray, with silver cup and spoon and a pretty doily, in which for refined patients I had much confidence, and which at once diverted their attention. When I sat down beside him he said once more to me rather quietly, "Can't eat, can't eat."

"Now, John, I made this just for you; it's awfully good, taste it."

Taking advantage of an open-mouthed objection, I slipped in a spoonful which he was obliged to swallow, greatly to his surprise; and so I quickly followed it with two or three more spoonfuls, and left the little tray for him to look at, and to help him to reason out why he could eat with another man's teeth.

Daily I fed him until he was able to take the regular hospital diet. While convalescent, and when quite himself, we had almost a quarrel. I wished to return the little silver watch, and he insisted upon my keeping it, this I refused until he declared that it was not good enough, and if I would not keep it he would send me a handsome gold one when he reached home. At last I consented to accept it as a keepsake from a boy friend, saying I would rather have it than a gold one. To my great regret, while galloping with a party through Petersburg, just after the capture, I lost it from my belt, with a bunch of rings made from buttons, and little tokens made by the boys from the bones of the meat in their rations.

Meanwhile I had written to his family and to his employer, Mr. Gibson, who wrote that if the boy could be taken home he would come for him. Immediately I wrote and explained to him what was necessary to procure a discharge or sick furlough. The former was soon obtained, as he was even then but a boy. Mr. Gibson came at once, and took the lad home in a most generous manner.

When, later, I went to Albany for an interview with Governor Fenton, I was entertained by his family; but John was not at home, and I have never seen him since.

During this period of the great Rebellion the most terrible battles of any recorded in modern history, were fought. After one of them, during which the same ground had been fought over repeatedly, now with success on the Southern side, now on the Northern, a flag of truce was sent in from the Confederate Army, asking for a cessation of hostilities that its soldiers might be allowed to bury their dead. The following poem, written by Amanda T. Jones, author of "A Psychic Autobiography," commemorates the heart-breaking incident. It will be found among her collected works entitled "Poems: 1854-1906."

A REBEL FLAG OF TRUCE

Let us bury our dead:
Since we may not of vantage or victory prate;
And our army, so grand in onslaught of late,
All crippled has shrunk to its trenches instead—
For the carnage was great:
Let us bury our dead.
Let us bury our dead.
Oh, we thought to surprise you, as panting and flushed,
From our works to assault you we valiantly rushed:
But you fought like the gods, till we faltered and fled,
And the earth, how it hushed!
Let us bury our dead.
So, we bury our dead—
From the field, from the range and the crash of the gun,
From the kisses of love, from the face of the sun!
Oh, the silence they keep while we dig their last bed!
Lay them in, one by one:
So we bury our dead.
Fast we bury our dead.
All too scanty the time let us work as we may,
For the foe burns for strife, and our ranks are at bay:
On the graves we are digging what legions will tread,
Swift and eager to slay—
Though we bury our dead.
See we bury our dead!
Oh, they fought as the young and the dauntless will fight,
Who fancy their war is a war for the right!
Right or wrong, it was precious—this blood they have

shed:
Surely God will requite,
And we bury our dead.
Yes, we bury our dead.
If they erred as they fought will He charge them with
    blame?
When their hearts beat aright and the truth was their aim?
Nay, never in vain has such offering bled!—
North or South, 'tis the same—
Fast we bury our dead.
Thus we bury our dead,
O, ye men of the North, with your banner that waves
Far and wide o'er our Southland, made rugged with
    graves,
Are ye verily right that so well ye have sped?
Were we wronging our slaves?
Well, we bury our dead!
Ah, we bury our dead!
And granting you all you have claimed on the whole,
Are we spoiled of our birthright and stricken in soul,
To be spurned at Heaven's court when its records are
    read?
Nay, expound not the scroll,
Till we bury our dead!
Haste and bury our dead.
No time for revolving of right and of wrong
We must venture our souls with the rest of the throng
And our God must be Judge as He sits overhead,
Of the weak and the strong,
While we bury our dead.
Now peace to our dead;
Fair grow the sweet blossoms of Spring where they lie;
Hark! the musketry roars and the rifles reply.
Oh, the fight will be close and the carnage be dread!
To the ranks let us hie:
We have buried our dead.

I found plenty of work to do, and attached myself to the
Ninth Corps especially, though visiting all the wards and
corps. I was invited by Mrs. Mayhew to work with her for

some weeks in the Maine State Agency. While there I was asked later, in the absence of Miss Gilson, of Lynn, Massachusetts, to take charge of the Corps d'Afric, but I soon found that the work was chiefly to look after refugee negroes, and to give them employment in laundry work, etc. Doctor Thomas Pooley was then in charge of that corps, and is now a distinguished oculist of Manhattan. I still see him, a very young man, resplendent in a new uniform with bright buttons, red sash, etc., as officer of the day.

Miss Gilson had come with Mr. Fay, General Superintendent of the Sanitary Commission, in the field, and formerly Mayor of Chelsea, Massachusetts, and she chose to work for the Corps d'Afric. That was quite as well conducted as any other corps. Miss Gilson was a dainty young woman, and, while in camp, wore a short pretty dress of grey cloth and a white kerchief tastily arranged over her dark hair and one about her neck. She had a pure soprano voice, and frequently sang army songs and hymns to the men, making them quite happy, and with a sort of reverence, they seemed to find her an angel of peace. In her earnest devotion, Miss Gilson remained too long ministering to typhoid patients from whom she contracted the fever, and at last was compelled to leave her chosen work and go to her home, still hoping to recover and to return to the patients of her corps. Her strength was not equal to the waste of that burning fever, however, and she died in her early womanhood, a sacrifice to her benevolence and patriotism as truly and honorably as the men who died on the field of battle.

I returned to the Maine State Agency, and found more special cases in the hospital than could be cared for by all the ladies. The United States Sanitary Commission was under the direction of the late J. Yates Peek, of Brooklyn, New York. The absence of sectarianism in their work gave them greater freedom than was found in the work of the "Christian Commission," which was conducted on "religious" principles. The latter, however, did a very large work under the direction of the late Mr. Henry Houghton, a distinguished oculist of Manhattan.

HELEN LOUISE GILSON

The large wooden chapel accommodated many hundreds, and here came preachers from all over the country, whose churches had contributed supplies and were anxious to know how their contributions were applied. Some ministers, from remote localities, were a great annoyance, having to be entertained by the Christian Commission, and wanting to regulate their donations according to the ideas of their own little parishes.

In the Maine State Agency the "mess" was at that time composed of Mrs. Mayhew and her lady assistants, with two or three convalescent officers. This pleasant party I was invited to join.

LIEUTENANT STANWOOD

Surgeon William O'Maugher, of the 69th New York Infantry, late coroner of New York City, a jolly Irish gentleman, and Lieutenant Stanwood, of Maine, with their wit and jolly talk were a great help to us, when we sometimes actually staggered to our tents, completely discouraged and exhausted. It was impossible to help all the sick "Boys," who were happy if we could give them only a pleasant word of cheer in passing. We frequently sat on the rough seats, leaning wearily on the plank tables supported on empty barrels; but their Yankee and Irish jokes, after a good meal, soon raised our spirits and we were ready to start again on the endless round among the sick.

One day at dinner, when I was particularly depressed, Doctor O'Maugher began with an extra brogue—"Yees all think a deal of Miss Smith, don't yees?"

"Well, I guess we do," said Lieutenant Stanwood, "and no one had better say anything against her."

"Well, if yees knew what I know about her y'd change yer mind." I was too tired to raise my head, and he went on: "Yees know about that Guffin boy she tuk care of? Well, she saved his life to be sure, but if ye knew the rist of it."

At last I said, "What's the matter with you, O'Maugher?"

"Well," he went on, "do ye know whin I wanted to put a fly blisther on the back of the boy's head, she wouldn't allow it, and for why do ye think? Well, she said it would spoil his looks for a corpse." This of course was followed with a shout of laughter which happily relaxed the tension of fatigue, and gave us courage to go on.

One morning when Doctor O'Maugher came to his "mess" he looked a picture of misery. "Why, Doctor, what's the matter?"

"Oh, it's a poor miserable cuss of a biped I am onyway."

"What makes you so unhappy?"

"Oh, it's just a miserable toothache that I have."

"Is that all? Well then, Doctor, you are only a bicusped after all."

"Be garry, it's right ye are," he laughed.

Mrs. Mayhew, a lady of much refinement, possessed a sweet soprano voice, and a few of us formed a chapel quartette. The singing was greatly enjoyed by the convalescents, especially as we took care to select good old time choruses in which they joined heartily. Planed planks on logs made tolerable seats, and a rough platform and a desk, lighted at night with lamps or candles, completed the arrangements of the great square room of unplaned boards, where, as Miss Nye remarked, we sometimes literally "sat under the drippings of the sanctuary."

Many evenings while resting from the fatigue of the day we sat outside the Maine Agency tent and sang army and other patriotic songs. Mrs. Mayhew with her rare sweet voice led the singing, and the chorus followed in our favorite songs of "Picking the Lint," "Tenting To-night," "We Shall Meet but We Shall Miss Him," "Star Spangled Banner," "Home, Sweet Home." The latter, however, caused many stealthy tears among the listening patients, so we often closed with something cheerful like "Yankee Doodle" or "John Brown's Body," etc. Owing to the quiet of the great hospital after dark the singing could be heard all over camp.

I was urged to take charge of the 2nd corps' diet kitchen in the absence of Miss Hancock, which meant to direct the soldier cooks, see to supplies, regulate hours and kitchen diet, etc., for four hundred convalescents.

Late one morning the head cook came to me saying, "It's time to begin dinner, and we have nothing but one little shoulder of lamb. The Commissary has not sent any meat or vegetables. What shall we do?"

This was a dilemma certainly. Four hundred hungry men must somehow be fed. All through the army at every camp, I believe, a temporary oven was set up during the halts, and excellent fresh bread was served daily. The government also supplied the very best of coffee, but this was not dinner. One must be equal to any emergency in the army. Telling the cook to get out his large cauldron and put into it the little allowance of meat to boil, I took an orderly with a wheelbarrow, and started on a forage among the agencies.

At Maine I begged some fresh vegetables. Ohio gave some canned meat, Indiana onions, New Jersey more canned goods. I sent the orderly with these to the cook, directing that everything be put into the cauldrons. We got another barrow load from the Pennsylvania, the Christian and the Sanitary

Commissions. This miscellaneous collection, when cooked and well seasoned, made "the best stew we ever ate," said the satisfied four hundred.

While at this diet kitchen some one stole my journal, money, and pass,—the latter the most serious loss, as no one could remain in camp without written authority. Happily, and to my surprise, when I applied to Surgeon Dalton as to what I must do, he said, "As I know of your good work in New York, Miss Smith, I will be happy to have you remain, but hope you will get a pass as soon as possible. The Provost Marshall, General Patrick, has authority higher than mine." The General was a strict disciplinarian, and had he known that my pass was lost he could have ordered me to "report to Washington at once."

Many strange things occurred in our daily work. While I was helping at the Pennsylvania Agency, a wild-eyed, simple-minded woman found her way to our tents. Twice before she had somehow either eluded the guards or had worried officers into giving her a temporary pass. She had come for "the bones of her son" who had died at White House Landing and was supposed to have been buried there in the early skirmishes of the war. Hoping to satisfy this persistent woman, Mrs. Painter, whose pass gave her authority, ordered a transport to take her with a detachment of men to the golgotha of her hopes.

We took the short sail and landed at White House Point, where it was thought the boy might possibly have been buried, as the men had been in a skirmish there. They tried to locate the body by driving down in many places a long slender iron bar, but no trace of it was found. The half-demented woman continued to declare that she would "yet hold those dear bones in her arms." She was finally persuaded to go home and come another time, which was the only way of relieving the hospital of her presence.

According to army usage everything movable might be taken from a deserted point. The White House was still standing in good order, with green lattice shutters, and Mrs. Painter directed the men to take them off and bring them to our tents, and a small summer house was added to our army property.

Chapter XII
City Point, Virginia—A Day in the Army

From a letter written Nov. 8, 1864

November 8th (Election Day) dawned upon a cloudy sky and misty atmosphere as peculiar to Virginia as is also the renowned and "Sacred Soil," after a few days' rain. This however, we observed after we had risen from our narrow hospital bed, which stood close by the side of the tent, that flapped in the face of the sleeper (or waker) as the wind rose or fell. The rain descended in torrents during the night, and all was damp as usual in our rag houses. Our sleeping apartment, or tent, the second one of the Maine Agency, was well stored with boxes of goods and delicacies for the sick, leaving little moving space. Late as was the season our tents were made comfortably warm with army fireplaces, and stoves, though the floors, made of broken boxes, were sometimes covered with mud. "Oh, were you ever into an Irishman's shanty?" I can not here describe our excellent agency which did more for the relief of soldiers, and more fully realized the idea of an army home, than any agency or commission on the field.

I accepted a pressing invitation from the New Jersey State Agent, Doctor Hettie K. Painter, to join a pleasure excursion. She, by the by, was a living example of the usefulness of a lady in the army, who can frequently effect more good by personal influence than would be allowed through regular channels.

Our pass being sufficient, we started in an ambulance with a clever driver, who drove around the camp and gave us an opportunity to see the extent of our hospital, having a capacity of over 9,000, and covering an area of twenty-five acres. We then crossed the Petersburg railroad, to which had been added a branch running directly into the middle of our camp for the more direct and comfortable conveyance of the sick and wounded.

DR. HETTIE K. PAINTER

We splashed on in the mud, through an opening in the fortification which protected the base. This defense extended about fifteen miles from the Appomatox River to the James River, and was a high, heavy earthwork, further protected by a deep ditch; earthworks having been found to be superior to stone fortification. How little did those at home know of the immense amount of labor here necessary! The pick and spade still played an important part in the warfare of our country.

Virginia was stripped of her artificial culture and bore on her bosom the scourge of war in the form of burned and felled woods, torn and altered roads, plantations deserted and laid waste, deeply furrowed fields turned into stony roughness and corduroy unevenness, which resisted even the indentation of wheels, and threatened frequent overturns. With all these marks of desolation, waste and destruction, Virginia was still beautiful in her woods and varied trees, now gorgeous in the oriental splendor of fall,—crimson, orange and pale yellow, with a background of the darkest green, fading into tan or sere and yellow,—with blended colorings indescribable, and hills receding in the distance. Near us— beyond the winding river and bayous, the dells and ravines and bluffs, which give to the quiet and beautiful scenery of this section its greatest variety and charm—was the Point of Rocks.

On we jogged in our springless ambulance, here passing an army train of supplies, or a load of logs for building winter quarters. Further on we ran our wheels into a loaded army wagon, drawn by six mules, but a dexterous turn brought us upon an evergreen bank, and we rode safely along, following a cavalry force. After riding about four miles, we came to Broadway Landing, (why so called I can not surmise), a depot at which General Butler's supplies were received and forwarded. Here we crossed the pontoon bridge, formed by placing flat-bottomed boats sidewise about ten feet apart, and fastening these by ropes and beams laid across from one boat to another, and heavy planks laid transversely across the beams. This makes a very simple, portable and strong bridge. The river at this point is less than a quarter of a mile in width, having a steep bank on either side.

On the eminence of the James River side of the Appomattox we came upon the marine artillery performing their drill. The rapidity with which they dismounted, and took to pieces and reconstructed their cannon seemed wonderful to an ordinary spectator. To the left we passed the spot said to be the veritable and memorable site of the historical incident of the saving of Captain Smith's life by Pocahontas. Her direct descendants, the Rolfs, give this as the locality, and the stump of a large oak tree at the extreme end of the Point of Rocks as the identical one,—now felled and lying down the bank,—under whose shade might have perished John Smith. And what then would the world have done for a scapegoat?

Still further to the left of us was the 18th Army Corps Hospital, and in the background, on the river bank, rose one of General Butler's great signal stations, 125 feet in height, to which were communicated from the smaller and hidden stations, the results of their observations, and whence they were transmitted to General Butler's headquarters. While at one of these smaller stations, we saw through glasses a train of nine empty cars, passing on the rebel road, which fact was immediately conveyed by a singular numerical motion of a signal flag. The flagman who gave this communication was remarkably expert in his motions.

After riding some three miles further we reached General Butler's provisional camp, then in command of General Graham. Only a part of the supplies were now forwarded to this point, the rest being conveyed by way of the James River. Here we stopped at the Hatcher farm. Judging from the number of barns and small houses scattered about, this must have been quite an extensive plantation. The owner and present occupant had taken the Oath of Allegiance, and having sent his slaves farther south, lived here quietly with his wife and three pretty children. But General Butler's vigilance would not allow him to leave his house or to speak to any one without the immediate attendance of a guard, who constantly walked before his door. Our cook supplied this rusty cavalier and family with the necessities of life, as if he were a northern "mud sill."

On the farm was quite a large negro cabin, built of logs, consisting of two rooms, one above the other. This was the telegraph station of this section and was under the supervision of the son of Doctor Hettie K. Painter, a lad of less than seventeen summers, who conducted the business as thoroughly as if it had been under the guidance or experience of grey locks. What strange stories passed over the lines from that mysterious little instrument, quietly working away on a side table as if only an ornament! These boy employees,—for our young friend Painter had assistance,—were all able to read by sounds which, to unpractised ears, seemed all alike.

In a large fireplace, over a log fire, Mrs. Painter made a camp kettle of cornstarch pudding, and George Washington, the contraband, boiled potatoes and fried the mutton chops; and with the addition of a few delicacies and good Java coffee, which we had carried with us, we had as good a dinner as hungry mortals could wish.

Dinner over, we gathered some of the beautiful autumn leaves, and rode on our way until we reached the renowned original "Crow's Nest" signal station. This was a huge tree seventy-five feet high, surmounting which was the "Crow's Nest," reached by rude ladders from one platform to another. This "Nest" resembled a thatched bird's nest on a large scale, about four feet square, and it was almost hidden by surrounding trees. A new skeleton station erected on the opposite side of the road left unused the "Old Nest." Several gunboats were lying in the river, below the banks of the James, ready for action.

Entering the ambulance, we continued our ride over hills and through ravines, at the risk of an upset, until we safely reached Dutch Gap, General Butler's famous canal. This was nearly completed at the cost of much time and labor, and only waited the blasting of a rock at the other end, to complete the work which would form an island of the narrow peninsula dividing the River James into two branches, to be connected by the canal.

Along both shores were heavy guns and strong fortifications, quite formidable, showing much labor and ingenuity. Despite the almost constant courtesy of interchanging shells passing overhead, the "Johnny Rebs," on one side of the river, and the Yanks on the other bank, had many quiet talks across the narrow stream. Talks like this were quite usual, and were even winked at by officers.

"Hello Yank, hev u'uns got any good coffee?"

"Well I guess! It can't be beat. Say, Johnny, how are you off for tobac?"

"O, we've got heaps of that. I reckon u'uns had better just float some of that coffee across."

"All right, Johnny, you get your tobac ready!"

By a little practice in watching the current, they became quite expert in floating across many exchanges besides the tobacco and coffee. They even risked being shot from their own side as deserters, and swam across after dark to enjoy a supper of "hot pone" on the "Reb" side, or hot coffee and some luxuries on the "Yank" side, where the sutler often consumed a month's pay at a time in selling good things to some "Boy in Blue."

Returning, we stopped only at the embalmer's, where many bodies were daily prepared to be sent to friends at home. The morbid fancy which is manifested by so many to possess dead bodies, especially those which have long laid buried, seems one of the most barbarous customs permitted in a civilized country.

We reached our hospital just as "night drew on her sable mantle and pinned it with a star." The camp fires and chimneys were throwing over the scene a bright and cheering glow. A good supper was prepared by our contraband Hannah, who, with a broad smile, declared in her own peculiar vernacular: "I's jes goin' gib you alls up; t'o't de rebs done got you dis time shoo nuff—I'se so glad."

We pressed our collection of leaves, and, after a short visit to headquarters and the ladies' tent where our stores were kept, we returned to "Maine" and laid away our weary bones, nearly shattered after a day's shaking over the corduroy roads. We were soon lulled to sleep by the 6th Army Corps singing "The Girl I Left Behind Me" and the humming of the singing mice which infected our tent.

CHAPTER XIII
Dorothea Dix

About this time I met Dorothea Dix, that masterful woman by whose persevering energies insane women were provided with suitable hospitals, instead of being confined with criminals, as was usual in the old days. She devoted her time, thought and influence to compelling the opening of decent asylums for these often refined, unfortunate women patients. Her good work, begun in this country, reached England and other countries, and was the beginning of that civilizing influence that no longer considered these unfortunates as subjects of divine punishment.

Miss Dix, a dignified lady, was then organizing a trained nurse corps. There were no trained nurses, or "Red Cross" at that time, but later we followed the Swiss movement. Miss Dix asked me to join her corps, but I declined, preferring to do independent work. I was glad, however, to turn over to her nurse corps, my three assistant nurses, knowing that with her they would receive pay for their services, which the Masonic Mission had falsely promised to us. Several young girls had been sent, with directions not to take money or clothing, as everything would be furnished. I had insisted on taking both. Some girls were stranded at Fortress Monroe, two or three of whom I succeeded in sending home safely. Three others, stranded and penniless, fell under the protection (?) of young officers. I then resigned my secretaryship of the Masonic Mission, with a threat to expose and have them arrested for false pretenses, but they disappeared in a night, and were never more heard of.

On the return of Miss Hancock to the second corps' kitchen, some red tape became tangled up, and, as I was invited to assist in the New Jersey and Pennsylvania Agency with Doctor Hettie K. Painter, I gladly accepted, and worked for the men of those states, though, each of the Agencies desiring my help, we all worked in the same spirit for all the "Boys."

A most interesting Pennsylvania case was that of a young captain who had received a thigh fracture while at the front at Petersburg. The leg had to be amputated so high that the artery could not be taken up, and it was impossible to close it in the usual manner. Consequently men were detailed to hold or press their thumbs ceaselessly upon the open artery, each man serving four hours at a time, although another was always ready to take his place in case the strain of holding so long in a cramped position should cause him to relax or faint. This was continued for weeks till the artery actually healed. I believe only one other such case occurred during the Civil war. While hastily passing through his ward one day, Lieutenant Stanwood called my attention to this officer.

Contrary to my intention of caring only for young boys, I felt it my duty to do what I could for this sufferer, whom I found in a very critical state, needing the utmost care to bring him through. Being a blonde, he was transparently white from loss of blood, and so weak that he scarcely tried to live. He had no interest in anything and no appetite. There was no time to be lost here, so I said—"Captain, you do not eat, I hear, and I want to make you something that you would like."

"I have no appetite," he replied feebly.

"Can you think of something you could relish?"

After a pause he said, "I think it's hardly worth your time. I shall not recover, but perhaps I could eat some barley broth if it is possible to get it."

Always strong on the optimistic side, I answered, "I think we can find some, Captain."

But where? Perhaps not nearer than Washington and forty or more hours away. Here was possibly a life to save. Beginning at the Sanitary Commission, at the head of the agency row, I went to each State agency in a faint hope of at least securing some substitute, but nothing could I find. Barley was such a simple thing; and now might save a life! I racked my brain to find some palatable substitute. As a last hope I went to the Christian Commission with my anxious inquiry, "Can't you remember if on your list of supplies some thoughtful man or woman has sent this now invaluable donation?"

Mr. Houghten said, "I seem to remember that about six months ago there was sent a little package marked barley, but how can we find it in this great store of supplies?"

"Oh," I exclaimed, "put on all your men to hunt for it; it may save a life worth saving."

To my delight, after a long search, a package of about four by three inches was discovered. Losing no time, I ran to my tent and started a few spoonfuls boiling. The surgeon had said not even salt could be allowed the patient, lest it should increase circulation and thus break open the artery scarcely healed.

At last with my special attractive little array of silver cup, dainty doiley, etc., I went to the poor captain. His refined face at once showed his appreciation of the neat service.

"Here's your barley, Captain," I said cheeringly; "let me feed you a few spoonfuls now, and I'll come back and give you a little more bye and bye. And, Captain, I shall leave it all here on this little table; don't let any one carry it off."

The poor, feeble cripple, who had not been allowed to change his position for many days, said—"They'd better not touch it!" and he fixed his great blue eyes on the tray with an air of defiance, pathetic to see. So his mind had something to guard, and this somewhat diverted his attention from the dying and suffering men about him. Next day the surgeon allowed a little salt, then a little butter, and at last a little meat. By this time his digestion would allow stronger food, and this was fortunate, for, though I had guarded every grain of the precious little package, it was almost exhausted.

I have often pictured to myself a kindly, country old lady in white cap and kerchief, whose prescience in sending this precious barley probably saved a life, and I wished that she could know it.

The captain lived, and went to Washington quite recovered, where he received a government leg (gratis) which fitted so well that he could jump off a moving car. He then went home quite well, having sacrificed a leg to his country. His temperate clean manner of living served him in an emergency and carried him over the crisis.

The mistaken idea of so many men, especially military men of that time, that liquor gives strength and courage, cost many an otherwise pure character his life in such an exigency.

By contrast with the above I will cite the case of Colonel Murphy, Sixty-ninth New York Infantry, second corps, a brave officer, worshipped by his men. He was a man of fine physique and robust appearance when I saw him, despite his fatal wound, a fracture of the thigh, similar to that of the Pennsylvania captain. To perform the amputation and carry him over successfully it was necessary to stimulate him and this was impossible, his body being already over-stimulated by the drinking habit to the last degree. I never before begrudged anything to a wounded man, but I knew that my choice brandy could not help him. He died without even a chance of being saved, mourned and regretted by his whole corps.

CHAPTER XIV
An Unexpected Ride

On a beautiful clear night, while still in the Corps d'Afric, a party of ladies and officers walked a short distance to a cabin where a negro preacher drew a large crowd. This man, though uneducated, was a wonder of natural oratory and eloquence. In addressing his admiring audience his vocabulary was remarkable, as he used some extraordinary sentences such as—"All the englomerated hosts of heaven."

While at this meeting an orderly came for me saying that a couple of officers from the front desired to see me at my tent. I found there two uniformed, mounted officers awaiting me, one of whom proved to be my old friend Captain Frank Dexter of the Engineer Corps.

The night was perfect in a mild atmosphere and a full orbed moon, and I was reminded of James' old time "Solitary Horseman," though here were *two* rarely handsome men of fine physique; and as they stood, holding their fiery steeds, they formed a romantic picture.

After a pleasant talk of home and friends they remounted, and with raised sombreros, their spurred horses dashed away to the clinking of sword and hoofs, while the bright moon rays glinted uniforms and accoutrements, till they passed under the shadow of the distant woods.

Captain Dexter had raised Company L of the Fiftieth Volunteer Engineer Corps early in the war, and still commanded that company at Petersburg front, and during many battles. After the close of the war, he became a successful physician, and in addition to his practice in New York City he held for many years the position of Police Surgeon.

CAPTAIN B. F. DEXTER

As some patients needed fresh milk, I started out boldly one afternoon, with an orderly carrying an empty pail and a basket of extracts and small supplies. We rode through the woods beyond our lines to a secesh house quite near. On the piazza were a pretty young girl and a young Confederate officer in full grey uniform. With them were two or three ladies. At first they were suspicious lest it was a ruse on our part to capture the young "reb," but a pleasant talk followed, and they were glad to exchange some quarts of milk for the small luxuries that they had been so long unable to secure, and to arrange an exchange of milk for such articles in the future.

We gave the sick rebel prisoners the same attention as our own boys. One asked why we were so kind to them, and I replied—"Why, don't you know we're feeding you up to make you well and then send you back so we can fight you over again." This greatly amused them.

A rumor spread through the camp that the rebel gunboats were coming down the James to capture the hospital. Much excitement followed as to what we women would do; should we try to escape or should we remain with the sick? We promptly decided to remain with our boys; but happily the gunboats did not come.

My only recreation was an occasional horseback ride, accompanied by a mounted orderly. As there was only one lady's saddle in camp, it was difficult to secure it. Two or three high cavalry saddles were altered so that women could ride, uncomfortably, on them. I once rode a horse from General Russell's headquarters at the Point, and found the animal quite unmanageable. He at once started for a run and it was impossible to check or hold him. I barely managed to hold on, winding the reins about my hands, and bracing myself in the too small saddle. We passed a hotel on the road where many officers were sitting, then General Grant's tent, and then dashed down the road over a pile of logs, nearly upsetting some soldiers at work there. With a sudden stop that nearly sent me over the horse's head the animal stood quietly in front of General Russell's open office window, where the General and his staff were consulting. They sprang up at the clatter and, gasping for breath, I said, "General, I didn't come to see you because I wanted to, but because I couldn't help it." And there was a general laugh. The check rein had been forgotten.

Another horse took me back very quietly, but for many days the strained muscles stood out like those of an athlete, and there was pain enough through my entire body to make me sympathize with a chronic "rheumatic."

We sometimes rode to U. S. Headquarters to see the drill and inspection of General Russell's colored brigade. General

Grant often stood beside his magnificent black horse at these inspections, and was very proud of the perfect drill of the negro infantry, whom he complimented, to their great happiness. These were the first colored troops I had seen.

According to General Butler's autobiography "The first regiment of colored soldiers was mustered in at New Orleans on August 22d, 1862. Better soldiers never shouldered a musket. They learned to handle arms and to march more readily than white men."

How little thought and justice has been given to the fact that, when enlistments began, and as the demand for Confederate troops became more imperative, even old men and boys were drafted into the Southern army,—for light duty perhaps. In some cases there was not a white man within many miles, and to the care and honor of these negroes, plantations of hundreds of acres were left that they might continue to raise food and supplies for their army. Despite the fact that thousands of these negroes had practically no restraint to fear, they cheerfully labored against a cause that even at that early day they felt was for their emancipation, and yet I never heard of an uprising that could not have been checked by helpless women. There was not a case of robbery, destruction of property or rapine among the faithful workers who became the protectors of Southern women and children.

In a sketch of the life of General Charles Halpin, (Private Miles O'Reilly) occur the following verses. "Sambo's Right to Get Kilt" was written to accustom the Northern soldiers to the presence of the negro. They had so strong a prejudice against the negro that they did not like him even to be killed in the company of white soldiers. Its effect was astonishing and its argument was unanswerable, and negro soldiers were ever after held in the respect due to their orderly conduct. General Butler considered them a necessity of Northern success, mainly due to the wonderfully skilled pen of General Halpin, who died at the early age of thirty-seven, at the height of literary honor.

GENERAL CHARLES HALPIN

SAMBO'S RIGHT TO BE KILT

Some tell us 'tis a burnin' shame
To make the naygars fight;
An' that the thrade of bein' kilt
Belongs but to the white.
But as for me, upon me sowl!
So liberal are we here

I'll let Sambo be murthered instead of myself,
On every day in the year.
On every day in the year.
And in every hour in the day,
The right to be kilt I'll divide wid him,
An' divil a word I'll say.
In battie's wild commotion,
I shouldn't at all object
If Sambo's body should stop a ball
That was comin' for me direct;
And the prod of a Southern bagnet,
So ginerous are we here,
I'll resign and let Sambo take it
On every day in the year.
On every day in the year, boys,
And wid none of your nasty pride,
All my right in a Southern bagnet prod
Wid Sambo I'll divide.
The men who object to Sambo
Should take his place and fight;
And it's better to have a nayger's hue
Than a liver that's wake and white.
Though Sambo's black as the ace of spades,
His finger a thrigger can pull,
And his eye runs sthraight on the barrel-sights
From under its thatch of wool.
So hear me all boys darlin',
Don't think I'm tippin' you chaff,
The right to be kilt we'll divide wid him
And give him the larger half.

Charles Graham Halpin
(Miles O'Reilly)

CHAPTER XV
Two Fiancées

We were all much interested in the case of a young lieutenant who had lost a leg and was slowly recovering. He had written to his fiancée that he was disabled, and would give her up if she so desired. He was now awaiting anxiously her reply.

Quite coincidently, at the other end of the ward was Major Hemlock, of the Forty-seventh New York Infantry, who had lost a leg and he, too, had written his fiancée offering to release her from her promise. As time went by without bringing a reply the lieutenant became very despondent. One day in passing I saw an unopened letter lying upon his breast and exclaimed: "Oh, lieutenant, your letter has come after all; but it is not opened! Shall I open it for you?"

"No," he answered in a despairing voice. "I know what it says."

Unable to persuade him to read his letter, and feeling quite sure that it must be favorable, I ran quickly to Mrs. Mayhew, of his State agency, telling her of the letter. She went at once to him, and in her sweet sisterly way at last induced him to consent to open the letter. His intuitions proved only too true. "Perhaps," the girl had written, "it would be best; we could still be friends."

Our indignation knew no bounds. The poor fellow sank rapidly and died a few days later of a broken heart. He was carried by his comrades, led by the funeral march of the shrill fife and the drum, to his soldier's grave in the woods, over which they fired the farewell salute.

During this time I was greatly surprised one day on visiting this ward to find Major Hemlock dressed and sitting up, looking happy and like another man. After a second glance I saw the cause of this change, for beside him sat a charming young girl who, in reply to his letter offering her a release, had started at once and succeeded in reaching him safely. The Major was soon able to travel and the happy pair returned to their home in Philadelphia where they were married.

MARY BLACKMAR

My friend Mary Blackmar, a medical student, enlisted as nurse, that she might serve her year in the field work with its wider experience, instead of in some regular city hospital. A year after the war she graduated from the Woman's Medical College, in Philadelphia, and assisted for a year in the dispensary with those wonderful pioneer women doctors Mary and Elizabeth Blackwell, in New York City. Miss Blackmar married, and finally, owing to ill health, was obliged to live in Florida, where she still practises medicine as Doctor Mary Blackmar Bruson.

In the winter of 1909 I found a little notice in the newspaper stating that Doctor Elizabeth Blackwell was still living near London at ninety years of age. About the same time I met a gentleman of my native city whose father (this name has escaped me) was the first reputable doctor to hold consultation with these remarkable women. This required courage, for at that time women doctors were considered bold intruders, "unsexed"—whatever that may mean—and why? Because they thought that it was time for women to know something about their own bodies and diseases.

One morning Miss Blackmar, quite excited, her dark eyes dancing with pleasure, ran into my tent exclaiming, "O, Colonel" (meaning me) "such a beautiful girl is in camp, you must see her! I don't know how she got here; but I can't stop a moment, I must run back to my patients."

Soon after, a graceful blonde was sent to us from headquarters to be entertained. She stated that, though English, she was in Edinboro when the news reached her that her brother was wounded at City Point, and she lost no time in sailing on the first vessel to America, where, perhaps owing to her good looks and persistence she succeeded in reaching our hospital. Meanwhile the brother had returned to his regiment, the Thirty-seventh Wisconsin, before Petersburg. I found means, however, to communicate with him, and in a few hours he pulled rein at our tent, having ridden many miles without a halt.

It soon developed that he was something more than a brother; though the girl claimed that this dashing, handsome young Englishman, Captain Robert Eden, was an adopted brother. He often got leave of absence that he might spend an hour with his fiancée, Miss Annie Bain, who became our friend and companion and, though taking no part in our work, remained with us during some months.

About this time our hospitality was taxed still further. An orderly brought a pleasant-looking woman and presented a note from Hospital Headquarters which read—"Please entertain Miss Mason, who is on her way South by 'flag of truce'…. She is secesh. Watch her."

Miss Mason remained a few days, and went South by first detachment of paroled rebel patients without any incident of interest.

Chapter XVI
The Story of My Pass

We were often annoyed by the calls of officers who, having little to occupy their time, could not understand how it was possible for us to be too tired to entertain them. They frequently called on me when I had many letters to write, and I would say to them: "Well, gentlemen, if it's any satisfaction to you to sit here while I write letters, I've no objection, but these home letters for the Boys are my first duty." They thought I should feel complimented by the calls of headquarters' officers, but I assured them I was quite aware that they had come to me only to kill time, when they had exhausted all other amusements.

It was really too much honor, and too much of a good thing when forty-five officers called on me in one week, some coming in from the front on short leave when all was quiet on the James, others from Grant's Headquarters, and from our Hospital Headquarters.

One evening I was very tired and three of these officers, fine looking men in full uniform, but slightly under the influence of liquor, annoyed me greatly. At "taps" I said significantly—"It's taps, gentlemen!"

"That does not concern us," one replied, "we can stay as long as we wish."

"General Grant himself could not stay in my tent after taps," I retorted indignantly.

They made no move to go, however. I arose and simply pointed to the tent opening, declining any reply to their remarks. They at last passed out in great indignation, and immediately one of these doctors began a petty persecution. Knowing that I had lost my pass he tried to have me sent to Washington. This soon became known in camp, and my friends set themselves to work to circumvent his unmanly spite.

He obtained an order from the Provost Marshall, General Patrick, by which all persons in camp not having passes should report at once to Washington. It was necessary, however, that he should notify personally any one so unfortunate as to have no pass. When he called at my tent I was never to be found, for whenever the doctor approached some one would say "Here comes C!" and I began a system of remarkable evolutions from one tent to another in the row, gliding back and forth, until he had to give up the search for the day.

Fortunately my good friend, Mrs. Doctor Painter, had made such a favorable report of me to General Grant's Headquarters that a pass was promised. The utmost diplomacy was necessary to gain time, but at last the pass was handed to me, secretly, on Thanksgiving eve, as we were decorating the mess hall for the coming feast.

The next day I was at home when Doctor C. called. I received him with much courtesy and said: "I hear, doctor, that you have called several times when I was not in. To what am I indebted for so much attention? Be seated."

The florid face grew redder, but I gave him no chance to speak, and in my most agreeable manner I talked and talked of everything I could think of, despite his many efforts to get in a word. Finally I grew tired of the fun, as were also some friends and listeners in the adjoining tent. Then, as if just remembering his attempts to speak, I said, "O, doctor, had you something to say to me?"

Growing still redder, if possible, and sitting uncomfortably on the edge of the barrel chair that I had insisted on his taking, he said, "O, only that an order is received that all persons not having authority must report to Washington. Er— er—have you a pass?"

"Doctor, you know that my pass was stolen." And I asked demurely what I should do.

With an air of exultation he sprang up and said— "Unfortunately, Miss Smith, you will have to report to Washington to-morrow."

Then slowly taking the pass from my pocket, I said

hesitatingly, "Well, Doctor, here is a paper that perhaps will help me," and I handed him the Grant pass.

"Headquarters Armies United States,
City Point, Virginia, March 16, 1865.

Miss Smith will be afforded all facilities that Army Commanders afford to other State Agents.

Free transportation will be given her on all Government steamers and Military Railroads. Guards and pickets will pass her accordingly.

By command of
LIEUTENANT GENERAL GRANT
T. S. Bowers, A. A. G."

I watched him in silence till he finished reading. His face was crimson and he said with a nervous giggle, "O, yes, er— I'll fix you up at medical headquarters all right!"

"Will you, indeed?" I replied, "I think I have fixed you. Now you may go," and he lost no time in going.

The laughter in the next tent must have reached him as he darted out and across the road to the hospital headquarters, where he exclaimed breathlessly: "D—— that Miss Smith. When I thought I had her all right she kept me on nettles for an hour, and then showed me an order from General Grant ranking me."

This soon became camp gossip, and he was jeered from one side to the other of the hospital.

CHAPTER XVII
Thanksgiving, 1864

Under Fire at Dutch Gap, Virginia

Greatly needing a day's rest from hospital work, I ordered an ambulance, good government horses and driver, and invited my guest, Miss Bain, and two reliable officers of the Corps d'Afric, stationed at General Grant's headquarters, City Point, to accompany us, and accept an invitation to dinner.

We started for the renowned "Dutch Gap," which had been excavated under the supervision of General Benjamin Butler, then in command of the Army of the James, and it was intended to compel the enemy to make a complete change of base.

A ride of seven or eight miles, through woods and over bumping corduroy roads and ditches, brought us to the James River, where we had been invited to a Thanksgiving dinner of goose (save the mark) on a commissary barge then anchored opposite the Gap. To my annoyance and Miss Bain's consternation, as she was interested only in Captain Eden, then at the front, we found ten or twelve officers in full dress waiting to receive us formally on the barge, when we arrived. It took a great deal of courage and not a little tact to get through that dinner creditably, while every man craved special attention.

After dinner we rowed on the narrow river to the monitor Onondaga and another war vessel near by. On board the Onondaga we encountered another crowd of naval officers, and were urgently invited to inspect these wonderfully constructed vessels which were stationed here to protect the Gap, and to prevent the rebel gunboats coming down the river.

GENERAL BENJAMIN BUTLER

We landed near this great excavation called "Dutch Gap," which was to be Butler's chef d'œuvre, viz., a channel cut across a long peninsula dividing the river at the end into two branches running almost parallel; in front of which the formidable Confederate mortars were continually sending shells all about this locality. A shell had dropped directly into the dredging machine, shattering it completely and it now lay on one side like a huge black mastodon. The channel lacked about twenty-five feet of successful completion, but owing to "orders" no further work was accomplished, and thus ended the great Dutch Gap strategy of Ben Butler.

The small row boat landed us on the muddy shore where little foliage remained to cover the denuded ground of the rough camp of an engineering corps and its guard. Despite the almost constant war courtesy of interchanging shots and shells, roaring on either side from the forts, and generally passing safely above the heads of "Yank" and "Johnnie" alike on each side of the river, they enjoyed many friendly talks across. Thus they broke the monotony of picket duty and gopher holes, while telling camp stories, true or otherwise, as the occasion suggested.

A story was told me that bears out on its face the imprint of possibility during the last days of the rebellion. A daring young "Reb," tired of life in the swamp and woods, with insufficient rations, while waiting for orders to advance, one dark night swam boldly across the narrow stream and was cordially received.

After enjoying a jolly evening around the camp fire, and especially, a good "square meal," he said to the Yankee boys, "You uns have plenty of good grub any way, and I'm about starved out. I say, Yanks, suppose you uns just surround me and capture me and march me up to headquarters as a deserter? I'd rather stay on this side and have good rations than to starve in the swamp on the other side."

This the "Yanks" did very cheerfully, and so another deserter was added to the Union army.

Our party started to walk around what was to have been Ferry Island, where the tortuous river made a sharp turn at the end, almost doubling on itself. An officer walking with me constantly changed from one side to the other. This surprised me and on my asking why he did this he replied "O nothing!" ignoring the question, though he continued changing sides as we walked on the uneven path. I insisted at last upon an explanation. He replied: "Well, you know the rebs are just across this narrow water in the woods, and it wouldn't look well if a lady should get a stray shot!"

"So you're making a target of yourself, Major, to gratify

my curiosity!" I was insisting on going back, when a "Johnny Reb" called across the stream in a pleasant tone, "Better take those ladies away!"

Mounting the great hill to look into the abandoned ditch where so much time and labor had been lost, we made a strikingly conspicuous group with the officers in uniforms, bright with the sun's reflections. Suddenly in the midst of witty talk and badinage a shell from the Rebel mortar shrieked over our heads, followed quickly by a second one with a deafening frightful explosion, and for a second we were stunned and almost paralyzed.

GENERAL BUTLER'S CANAL AT DUTCH GAP
(By kind permission of Harper's Weekly: Appeared Febr. 5, 1864.)

But not a moment was lost. An officer on either side grabbed the hands of Miss Bain and myself and "sans ceremonie," ran us quickly down the hill until we were safe in a large bomb-proof gopher hole, where we stopped for breath. These gallant officers carried a quantity of "Sacred Soil" on their spotless white trousers and polished boots. Here we waited while the shells continued to fall at some distance.

A large hole had been dug in the side of the hill where a plank floor and roof had been made to prevent falling in. This served as a mess room, while around the side of the high bluff, in small gopher holes, men hived like ants in their earth hills.

Hospitality suggested that a supper be prepared for us, and it was spread on planks with newspaper tablecloth, tin cups and plates, and two-tined forks. An old aunty cook waited on us, and served some rather weighty biscuit. The "pièce de résistance" at this supper and also at the barge dinner, was a rather opaque tumbler filled with peppermint sticks, which had been procured from the sutler.

The firing continued, and shells struck the water in the only channel by which we could return. Night was coming on, and I was at a loss to know what to do. Not wishing to alarm Miss Bain, I took an officer aside and consulted him.

They would do the best they could for us with only gophers for shelter, if we wished to pass the night there. If we attempted to cross the river it must be at our own risk, as the firing would probably continue until nightfall.

I decided at once for myself, but Miss Bain was my guest and must be given a choice. The agency people had always been careful to avoid even an appearance of evil. "Should we brave the comment of staying all night in a strange camp, or must we risk our lives in attempting to escape the shells falling on our route?" Without a moment's hesitation the courageous girl said firmly and briefly, "I'd rather risk the shells and drowning."

A boat was ordered at a pistol's point, and the poor pallid rower was so frightened that he could scarcely hold the oars. We got in with only our two escorts; the others were evidently not at all eager to accompany us back, but stood behind the hill anxiously watching our dangerous passage.

As we passed close by the Onondaga and her companion nothing living could be seen on these fully manned monitors. They had closed down their steel decks while the shells struck, ricocheted and fell harmlessly into the water like great marbles, as we passed by. A few feet farther on was the barge where we had dined with our military escort and where busy hands had helped us into the boat. It was now as deserted as if never occupied, the men had fled for safety to the woods. As we neared the muddy bank one shell struck a few feet astern of our boat, sending up a column of water like a geyser; another passed close overhead with its uncanny blood-curdling shriek, and struck the shore just ahead of us, where it exploded, driving pieces of shell and mud in every direction.

On reaching the mud shore, it was almost impossible to mount the rough improvised dock or float. However, our escorts pushed and we climbed up, with no formalities, and without loss of time. At first I could not see my ambulance, but soon it came out of the woods with the frightened horses dashing down the hill. The driver as he turned, shouted, "I can't stop, you must get in somehow!" Certainly it was "somehow" that our officers tumbled us into the rocking ambulance as it turned and dashed wildly back into the woods.

No word was spoken until the driver checked his mad race and we were out of range of the still falling shells, and could congratulate ourselves on our narrow escape. We reached camp at twilight, a little excited by our adventure, but quite the heroes of the day; and we resolved that it would be a long time before we again wandered out of camp.

Since writing the above experience I have found in General Butler's autobiography, the only historical statement of that strategical attempt on the James River, and it confirms my memory. This work was considered of the greatest military importance then, and if accomplished as designed, it would, without doubt, have given to our navy and land forces the control of the river almost directly in front of Richmond. This would have shortened by several months the acute warfare by which hundreds of lives were sacrificed.

That it failed when all was prepared to blow out the bulk head, and admit our monitors through the canal, was due to the fact that the original Commander (Smith) was ordered elsewhere, and that the new Commander begged Commodore Ludlow not to open Dutch Gap because he feared that the enemies' fleet would come down, and he did not know that he could sustain the attack, etc. This Commander was dismissed for cowardice later, when he took fright while the enemies' fleet attempted to come down the river, and, without any attempt at defense, ordered the Potomac to make all speed, and only stopped when he knew that an accident to the Confederate vessels had prevented an assault on the United States Headquarters at City Point, which might have destroyed the camp and involved an entire change of base.

That one finds little allusion to this engineering attempt is doubtless due to the fact that most histories of that time were written by West Point officers, who gave few details outside their own personal experiences; and regard for the gallant volunteer service was seldom admitted and too often entirely ignored.

General Butler often fell under this ban, and he lost no opportunity, when possible, of publicly showing the superior education in tactics of the volunteer officers and men under his command during the war.

In this personal sketch I do not attempt to write history; but give only a few selections regarding the expectations then known to many in that locality of the James River. I have given only a few selections from "Butler." These any one may verify, and in doing so will come across many other details of interest.

"Captain Melantha Smith, of the navy, assured me that it was impossible for his monitors, drawing sixteen feet of water, to get up further than Trent's Reach. We made a reconnaissance to devise a plan by which he might ascend the James with his vessels, then lying at a point called Dutch Gap.

"Here is a peculiar formation, the river running up by Trent's Reach, bends very sharply to the right and returns again, in an elongated horseshoe, so directly that while it has passed over a distance of over seven miles, the waters of the river at a depth of twenty-five feet, approach so nearly, that there is only about four hundred and twenty-five feet from the water on the other side across the neck at Dutch Gap to twenty-five feet of water on the lower side, so a canal wide and deep enough for our gunboats to get through, would require a cut less than four hundred feet long, sixteen feet deep, sixty feet wide at the bottom and ninety feet at the top.

"After having made a reconnaissance with Captain Smith, then in command of the naval forces of the James River, I went down to City Point and asked General Grant and Chief Engineer Barnard to come up with us to examine the premises. This they did and made a careful examination of the point. This was known as Dutch Gap for the reason that some enterprising German had cut quite a gap in undertaking to build a waterway through, many years before. We came to the conclusion that it was a desirable thing to do, and General Grant directed me to undertake it.

"Exploration proved it to be of very hard limestone and

gravel; in it was imbedded petrified wood, whole trees being turned into a very friable stone, easily broken.[1]

"The enemy, appreciating the importance of this strategic undertaking, and finding that we could not be reached by direct fire of their artillery, erected some mortar batteries on the other side of the James River. At a mile and a half distance it is not easy to drop a shell with any certainty into a space three hundred feet long by ninety feet wide.

"The first thing to do was to station a couple of well instructed men at points from which every shell could be watched during its wild flight. These observers after a little practice could tell almost precisely where the missile would land—whether it would come into our excavation. While the men were at work, these men were on the watch, and if a shell was likely to fall in our way, the watchmen would call out "Holes," whereupon the men would rush into the bomb-proofs, and come out again and resume work as soon as the shell had struck or exploded without harm."

Dutch Gap has since been dredged out and is a main channel for commerce between Richmond and the outer world. The waters of the James River being directed by the canal, no longer flow around through any depth at Trench Reach, and that which was the former channel of the river will soon become marsh land. Dutch Gap is the only military construction of all that was done by our army, which remains of use to the country in time of peace;—a monument to its projector and constructor,—one of "Butler's failures."

My army friend of 1864, Mr. J. Yates Peek and his wife, within a few years, have sailed through Butler's Gap, remembering the days of its intended strategy and the great disappointment when the navy caused its failure.

---

[1] I still have a piece of this black stone picked up at this point, at the time of my visit there in the year 1864. I have also an excellent cut of the gap at this time, better in some details, I think, than the pictures in the Butler Autobiography.

Chapter XVIII
Domestic Life in Camp and Other Incidents

In Pennsylvania and New Jersey State quarters combined, we had three good-sized connecting tents; and later the little New York house was added.

Our kitchen was generally run by Hannah, a rather incompetent contraband, with great wondering eyes and slipshod feet. There were many such about camp, girls and women as well as men and boys—anxious to work for shelter and food, but without knowledge of the value of money, which they generally squandered at the sutler's for some trifle such as candy, or something to eat. Sufficient for the day was their evil tempter.

A good cooking stove was a great comfort, and Doctor Painter, an excellent cook, made our mess appetizing. The agents were expected to get their sustenance from State supplies, and we could buy from the Commissary Department good bread and coffee. Our table was made of boards resting on barrels, and sometimes we were quite stylish, having a white tablecloth instead of newspapers. Our dishes, mostly of tin, served quite well for hungry, hurried appetites.

Our reception tent, which was the largest, had at first a bunk in one corner where the rain sometimes percolated through the canvas walls, and one morning,—my pillow touching the wet wall of the tent,—I found my head in a little puddle of water. But I was in better health, if possible, than before. We laughed at these happenings, also when the rain ran in streams over our ground floor and at night we were obliged to sit resting, or writing by the light of candles stuck in bottles, with our feet on logs to keep them dry. Meanwhile a log fire burned cheerfully in the rough mud and log chimney. A barrel was placed on top for draught. It sometimes caught fire, but some one always managed to discover it, and knocked it off without setting fire to the canvas roofs. Our barrel chairs were not luxurious, but, like everything in camp, they served their purpose.

Though our tents were not transparent, the candle distinctly silhouetted our forms on the walls as we sat talking with friends, so that passers could recognize visitors and perhaps wait for a more favorable time to call. During the day our tent flaps were always open hospitably. Agents and officers often visited and talked of home, friends, comforts, etc., while each was always ready to assist in an emergency. Convalescents often got leave to come for some luxury or necessity; they craved fruit and vegetables, especially onions, and one so craved this luxury that he offered me fifty cents for one. Of course it became a gift, and one that was greatly enjoyed.

The wife of the Ohio agent, a pretty brunette with long black curls and black eyes, became very ill. Their small tents were not comfortable. All the ladies helped in many ways to make her limitations less trying. We were fearful of a sad ending as she lay helplessly weak for many days, but youth and courage, with good care, at last put her upon her feet again quite well.

An extremely annoying encounter occurred while I was with Mrs. Painter in my little house attached to another tent. One evening, with considerable clatter, an officer, followed by his orderly, halted at my door and knocked for admission. I saw at once that this otherwise fine young man, from Brooklyn, was under the influence of liquor. There was no escape and I must, if possible, get along peaceably with him.

My friends in the next tent could hear every word and could have helped me to get rid of him, but they thought it a good joke to get me cornered, while they laughed and quietly enjoyed the interview.

"Miss Smith," mumbled the visitor, "I'm so glad to see you. I told the fer-rers I'd give fifty dollars for an introduction to you, when I saw you on the ch-cha-chapel platform singing just as if you didn't care fu-fur any body."

I could think of no plan to get rid of him, and still hoped

my friends would come to my rescue.

"Oh, Miss Smith," he went on, "I wish I had a ba-ba-badge like yours. Couldn't you give it to me?"

Thinking to escape his effusions and to hasten his exit, I took off my precious Lincoln mourning badge and handed it to him. But he grew more persistent, saying:

"Wouldn't you just pin-pin it on?"

In silent indignation and protest I did so, to his great satisfaction. Then as his speech grew more indistinct, he added: "W-w-when I tell the ferrers that M-Miss Smith put-put that on, they'll all be ravin' jealous!"

I do not remember how at last I got him out of the little house. I saw his orderly help him to mount a superb horse that had impatiently pawed the ground since he entered.

My indignation passed for little above the shouts of laughter at my discomfiture that for once I was caught in a dilemma.

But this recalcitrant young officer received a startling communication on the following day which, doubtless, caused a permanent revulsion of admiration.

The wife of an officer, with her four year old girl, was very anxious to join her husband at the front. Knowing that I held a pass, she persuaded me to take her to the camp, which might have made me considerable trouble, as she could not get permission from Headquarters. Being willing to help her, if possible, I sent for an ambulance and driver, and we started over the corduroy roads, ditches, ruts and mud,—a foot deep in some places,—occasionally in danger of being overturned, as we rode at times partly on one wheel or two, rarely on four. In a sudden lurch this mother so lost her head with fright that she raised her feet and shot out on one side into the "Sacred Soil" of Virginia, quite up to her knees. I grasped the child and flung myself with her on the opposite side, thus righting the ambulance, and feeling little sympathy for the mother who forgot her child, though her feet were completely covered with mud. We found her husband in camp, and I left them quite happy in their tent before Petersburg.

One of our surgeons owned a superb black horse that was so intelligent, one could not pass him without petting him. This he greatly enjoyed, and he showed that he remembered me. His handsome owner remarked, "I'm soon going to take you for a ride on him."

"O, you are, indeed. I believe it takes two to make an engagement, and I have reasons for not wishing to ride with you," I replied. "Good morning!" and so I left him greatly incensed.

Officers were constantly riding about our camp, and among them was Doctor Weir Mitchell of the cavalry, now the distinguished nerve specialist of Philadelphia, and author of many scientific works as well as novels. He often dashed down our row on a spirited horse, his long hair floating back, while his yellow-lined cape, thrown over his shoulder, made him a conspicuous figure.

Doctor Olmstead, of the 69th Regiment, a Brooklyn man, had received a wound in his foot from a spent ball, and for some time limped quite comfortably about camp. We much enjoyed his occasional calls and his kindly courtesy. I wear, on occasion, a silver trefoil of the 2d Division, 2d Corps, to which he belonged, made from a silver quarter (scarce in those days) and urged upon me by a grateful boy patient. Doctor Olmstead was kind enough to send it to Washington and have it made. It is now a much valued relic.

On Christmas Day, 1864, Mrs. Painter, wishing to make a pleasant surprise with home-made cheer for her son, Hettie K. Painter, who was still in charge of the telegraph at Hatch's Run, again invited me to accompany her.

After the usual bumping over corduroy and other bad roads near the point, we found him in his little improvised office and living room. Doctor Painter with the assistance of a cheerful contraband helper soon prepared a surprisingly comfortable Christmas dinner, which was greatly enjoyed by our little party.

During this homely visit, Hettie Painter remarked to me, "Miss Smith you are always looking up some souvenir of the war, here is something that you may appreciate. This is a telegram from General Sherman, received here this morning en route, and I immediately forwarded a copy to President Lincoln in Washington. It is therefore a copy of the message before it was despatched to the President."

Much pleased with this souvenir, now a relic of that wonderful conquest, I have preserved it carefully. Some months since I presented it to the U. S. Grant Post of Brooklyn, and by them it was neatly framed and is now in the fine military museum of that post's relics. The following is a verbatim copy:

"The United States Military Telegraph
Savannah, Ga., 23, 1864
Via Fortress Monroe, 25.

To his Excellency, President Lincoln:
I beg leave to present you as a Christmas gift the City of Savannah, 150 guns and plenty of ammunition; also about twenty-five thousand bales of cotton.

W. T. SHERMAN,
Major General."

I mailed it to my home, writing on the back, "This despatch was just received by a telegraph reporter. It is the first reliable original telegram."

Chapter XIX
Love In Camp

Miss Annie Bain was still with us, and had become my friend, and my companion, when time permitted. She made a restful change in the monotony of daily incessant hard work when, except for letter writing or in some extreme case when a dying soldier called us out, we remained during the evening in our tents.

Impossible as it seemed for a woman without pass or authority, Miss Bain succeeded, with little difficulty, in reaching City Point. A little tearful entreaty from a beautiful young woman has often moved the heart of the strictest disciplinarian. Upon reporting at City Point to that ogre of the department to all stragglers and irregulars, General Patrick, he gave her protection and permission to remain until her brother should receive his furlough.

Meanwhile Captain Robert Eden, of the 37th Wisconsin Regiment, whose wound was but slight, had returned to his post, and was at the front. There Miss Bain was not allowed to follow. But word soon reached the Captain, and in a day or two after Miss Bain's arrival he dashed into camp on his fine bay horse, well dusted after his long ride. He was a six-foot, broad-shouldered, ruddy young Englishman, and was brimming over with anticipation and happiness.

The first meeting, however, betrayed the secret that "Bob" was the lover for whom this courageous girl had braved the perils of the ocean, and the dangers and uncertainties of a country at war. Miss Bain explained that "Bob" was her adopted brother, and she feared that he might die of his wounds if left to strangers, and so she had come hoping to take care of him.

MRS. R. C. EDEN

Captain Eden was promised a furlough and promotion but it was long deferred. It was decided that when the promised furlough came they would go at once to Washington for the marriage ceremony and for a honeymoon trip. Bob managed to get an occasional pass from his regiment, then in camp before Petersburg always ready for orders to advance for action.

COL. R. C. EDEN

It was well that Annie had succeeded in gaining from the

department of the Provost Marshal General, the privilege of remaining till Captain "Bob" should receive his furlough. And well it was that the words took that form, for three months passed and yet no furlough came, while "Bob" stormed and laughed, impatient, though happy in anticipation, while he continued to make flying visits to our quarters.

At last envy, loving a lofty mark, and not knowing the goodness and purity that were her guide, sought some explanation of Annie's quiet reserve which ungratified curiosity magnified into many vague surmises, and which were now taking the form of unpleasant rumor. Annie at last became conscious of the false position in which she appeared, and which was chiefly due to the presence in camp of a handsome young lady having no ostensible object for her stay.

Thanksgiving and Christmas passed with good dinners sent to the soldiers by the liberality of citizens, who also sent agents to assist in the distribution. Some accessories were supplied by the Hospital Department, and the ladies in camp, with much taste and ingenuity in arrangement and decoration of the stockade dining barracks or "mess hall," produced a really fine display, and gave to the ever unsatisfied convalescent soldier "a good square meal."

Meanwhile, though with womanly tact Annie endeavored to hide her anxiety, my sympathy soon discovered "the worm in the bud" that saddened the eye and paled the cheek of the fair girl. Something must be done, and that quickly. A bold thought came to me; but extreme cases require heroic treatment, and after all we can but fail.

With assumed indifference, breaking in upon one of her reveries, I said, "Annie, you are unhappy."

"Why no, Miss Smith, I am very happy," she answered trying to believe herself sincere.

"Well, never mind, I know all about it, Annie, and am very sorry too, but mean to help you if you will allow me."

With an expectant yet alarmed glance she exclaimed: "Why, what can you do?"

"No matter; but will you answer truly one question? In the first place you know it is necessary for me to start for

Albany at once to see Governor Fenton, and Mrs. Painter is called home on business; and you cannot be left here alone. You are distressed and unhappy, and with reason; Bob cannot go to Washington, as you well know, and now please answer without reserve. If Bob should wish to marry you here, in camp, will you consent?"

"Why, we could not be married here," she exclaimed.

"That can be managed if you will give your answer."

"Well, yes, I would," she replied reluctantly.

But womanly delicacy instantly repented and she added, "O, I would not for the world have Bob think I am in the least bit of a hurry."

"Don't think of that! He shall never know of this conversation unless you are willing; and you will have nothing more to do about it."

In the course of the next hour a letter was written to Bob, in which her real position was plainly set forth, adding the very unpleasant suggestion, that should he fall in the expected battle, the poor girl would be doubly miserable. And further, if, after calm deliberation, he wished to place her rightly in camp, and marry her here in the Field Hospital, it was only necessary to telegraph at once and come to City Point at five P. M. to-morrow, and it should be done with every arrangement made.

A rare chance had brought to our tent that day an officer of Captain Eden's regiment, by whom the letter was at once dispatched. Little suspecting its importance, he delivered it at midnight to his comrade, as he dreamed by his camp fire of the long deferred day when Annie should be all his own. Astonishment and indignation, at the thought of an injustice to the brave girl who had dared all in her devotion to him, at once cleared away the mists of romance that had surrounded his bright visions of the future.

By the first trembling of the morning wires came the telegram, "All right, on the way to City Point on horseback." This was shown to Annie, who trembled with anxiety and mortification lest he should think her deficient in maidenly reserve; but we laughed away her fears and said nothing. Still I would not take any decisive action in this emergency until he came and assured me of his earnest wish. So the morning wore slowly on until nearly noon, when Hannah "the great-eyed" stumbled into the tent,—her usual manner of entering,—saying, "Lor, Miss Smith, Mass Bob dun come ridin' way down de road, ready to broke him neck."

I slipped quietly out of the tent as he dashed up on his fine horse, well flecked with foam, and pulled rein for the first time in fifteen miles of Virginia road! Covered with dust, but without a thought of fatigue, he sprang to the ground and, with a hearty grasp of my hand, exclaimed, "Colonel, you're a trump! Never would have thought it possible!" and with a significant gesture he whispered, "Do you mean it?"

"Certainly!" was the suppressed reply, for tents are all ears.

Laughingly he continued, "Couldn't get a pass so came without it. Ha, ha! must be back to-night!"

"Well, there's no time to lose; go and persuade Annie, and be ready at five P. M. sharp. It is now nearly noon, and all is yet to be done."

With a bound, Bob was by Annie's side, while she, half alarmed, was yet too happy in his presence to speak the thoughts that caused her heart to leap with a strange emotion.

It must have been like some wild dream when I said "Annie, Bob has something to say to you alone; so for once he may enter our sanctum." And unpinning the flap of the little tent attached to a larger one, they disappeared within.

Gathering my scattered thoughts, I ejaculated, "Let's see, what first? Ah, here comes Mary Blackmar. I want you to put on your other dress and be here at five P. M."

Her fine hazel eyes dilating in wonder, she exclaimed, "What ails you, Colonel?"

"Nothing, only we are going to have a wedding in camp, and you're to be second bridesmaid for Annie."

"Impossible!"

"Can't be helped. Manage your work somehow. You must come just the same, and Mr. Peek is to stand with you. Good-bye,—we're off for the clergyman. Remember, five P. M., and, one moment,—not a word in camp."

Meanwhile Sister Painter had sent for her orderly and ambulance, into which I quickly sprang while she called out with cheery significance, "Good luck! Good luck!" and the impatient pair of grey horses dashed off through camp to the Cavalry Corps Hospital nearly a mile distant, to secure the services of Chaplain Mines, the only Episcopal clergyman in that department.

An unusually cold air chilled us as we drove up to the tasteful little office of the Chaplain. His orderly saluted, and awaited my order. "Please ask the Chaplain to step here as quickly as possible."

To my consternation he replied "Chaplain Mines went North this morning!"

Dumbfounded at this news, and greatly distressed, I hardly knew what to do next. The driver was shivering, and evidently in doubt too, as he asked "Where shall I drive now?"

"To—to—O, I don't know—that is, drive back."

What could be done? Away we sped and my perplexity increased, for I well knew that none but the Church of England service could give sanction to this pair in matrimony. "O, I have it, drive to the Christian Commission."

In fifteen minutes we found Mr. Houghton, head of this commission. "Do you know," I cried breathlessly, "you are to be best man at a wedding this afternoon, and I'm to be first bridesmaid, and—well—there is no Episcopalian clergyman in this camp? You must help us out of this dilemma. Will you not ask one of your ministers to perform the service by the Episcopal form?"

With a twinkle in his keen gray eye he remarked "I think I shall order a straight jacket, and—"

"Never mind! Order what you like, but not a word in camp, or we shall have more assistance than we desire. Though this must not be done in a corner, yet one from each post will suffice. If it gets out we might have hundreds. We ladies will represent the States, Mr. Peek the Sanitary Commission, and you, Mr. Houghton, the Christian Commission, and—at five P. M. you'll know the rest, for there is yet much to do. I'm off now for General Patrick."

Again we dashed off over the rough frozen roads, this time in the direction of General Grant's Headquarters, near the James side of the Point. The day was intensely cold, and only a guard was visible, marking his frozen beat. As we approached he called an orderly, who immediately appeared and received the message "Ask General Patrick if he can be seen."

"General Patrick went North yesterday!"

"How long will he remain?"

"Till to-morrow night."

Match-making was becoming a doubtful experiment. "Has everybody gone North?" I dubiously inquired.

The orderly suggested "The General's adjutant, Captain Beckwith is here."

"Oh, indeed, I don't know *him* except by sight; a young man and good-looking. If only he wasn't. Wonder what General Grant would say if he were asked!" But a consideration of the cares of that overworked public servant saved *him*.

At last, in desperation, I said, "Ask the Adjutant if he will please step here for a moment," inwardly adding "If we do not perish with cold in this attempt, we might hereafter make our headquarters at the North Pole!"

Captain Beckwith came out of the office and politely waited my request. A poor attempt at indifference was not helped by my hesitating words—"Captain, I—er—I wish to speak to you privately. Is your office occupied?"

He replied gravely and politely, "There are officers now in my tent."

"Well then, will you please step into the ambulance, as it is necessary to have your advice and assistance."

Apparently anticipating a torpedo, when only a flag of truce was offered,—rather dimly to be sure,—he cautiously took his seat without a word.

How shall I quickly explain? Why doesn't he say something—not a word—one or the other must drop preliminary caution, or the words will freeze on our lips. So I blundered out "Are you engaged at five P. M.?"

He replied that he thought he was. Whereupon I told him the whole story, and he soon changed his plans.

"As General Patrick is away," I said, "will you come and witness the ceremony?"

"But I'm afraid it——"

"Nonsense, Miss Bain has remained by permission of

General Patrick. We wish you, as his representative, to give your countenance and endorsement to the affair."

Now he was interested, and finally agreed to be on hand. Away we hurried back to the Christian Commission, and found we had only two hours left.

After returning from the Cavalry Corps Hospital I found Bob within the tent standing alone with a gloomy and discontented expression upon his face. I took the alarm and said quickly: "There is something wrong, Bob. If you are intending to marry Annie because you think you must, don't do it, she's too good a girl to be forced upon any man in that manner. Now is your time to retreat. What is the matter?"

With a merry laugh, Bob said soothingly: "There, there, Colonel, you are wasting ammunition. Why, don't you know that nothing in the world could make me so happy as to marry the dear girl, and if we succeed I can never repay this great kindness, so don't waste time or thought on that point!"

But the cloud once more passed over his face. What did it mean? Half repenting the new role, I was hurrying away, when a neglected message came to my mind, and I called out, "O, Bob! Major Baker, before going North, requested me to say he had left forty dollars for you with the sutler at the Point!"

The cloud vanished, as he sprang up and exclaimed: "Did he? Bless his old heart! I must run down and get it."

"Why, how delighted you seem; one would think it was a fortune."

"O no,—but you see—er well, it is—all right now."

The cloud was explained! How mortal we are! The poor fellow was "dead broke" and of course had no fee for the clergyman. This seemed a small matter, but for several months that ever-welcome individual, the Pay-master, had not reported to the consequently bankrupt "front," so there was nothing to borrow, for as long as a dollar remained in camp, it was the common property of the "Boys."

On the road shortly after, we met Bob beaming as a sunflower, radiant in a brand new pair of yellow buckskin gauntlets, high cavalry boots, freshly blacked, hair and beard barbered, dust swept off his faded uniform, and with a clean paper collar. The owner of this elegant wedding attire called out merrily—"How are you progressing, Colonel?"

"Finely," was the brief though hardly conscientious reply, which was scarcely verified on reaching the Christian Commission again, when Mr. Houghton said: "I can find no one willing to perform that ceremony!"

Descending from the ambulance and passing into the quarters occupied by Rev. Mr. and Mrs. A., I asked the former to assist in giving away the bride, which he at once consented to do. But the most important character was still wanting.

"Ah, Rev. G., will you not as a home friend kindly perform this service?"

"With pleasure by the Methodist form, but I have conscientious scruples about using another service!"

"Well, please send some one else."

This one had scruples too. This seemed an absurd prejudice to stand in the way of so much happiness. The fourth or fifth minister was "perfectly willing" but hadn't the least idea of an Episcopal service. Verily this was the pursuit of happiness under difficulties. But I rejoiced then that all obstacles seemed to be at last overcome. Grateful to this liberal Methodist minister I thanked him and said: "If you are willing, please wait a moment."

Running quickly to Mr. Houghton, he soon found a prayer book and a key,—not of the book but of the chapel door. How the time flew! Four hours and thirty minutes gone; only twenty-five minutes left! The minister and I entered the chapel, where I explained to him the form of the Episcopal service, and to save time enacted the part of the groom, the bride and the other necessary characters. Much delighted with this service, he was proceeding finely when we came to the giving of the ring. "Oh, how about the ring," he asked. Here was another dilemma. Shades of the Goddess of Matrimony! A ring! and in camp, where jewelry was conspicuous only by its absence! My only ring, a garnet cluster, would not serve for a wedding ring, yet a ring must be had. Leaving the reverend absorbed in his part I ran to the tent again and rushed in upon Bob and Annie, happy and quite oblivious of time, forgetting almost my presence, and that it was for *their* marriage, that I had stirred up every department in the great hospital and the U. S. Headquarters.

In a tone of dismay I exclaimed: "What shall we do for a ring? It is impossible to find one in this last moment."

But to my intense amazement and great relief Miss Bain in a most matter of fact manner replied, "Why, I have a plain ring in my valise." This she placed in my hand, and I gave it to Bob, who deposited it safely for the auspicious moment. So I sped happily away, calling back, "Be ready in five minutes!"

And now we must marshal our forces and prepare for the silent wedding march, for which no Mendelssohn or Lohengrin could give sweet music, and which must be under cover to avoid attracting attention. At this moment an orderly hastily entered saying, "Mr. A. is very sorry, but a telegram has ordered him directly to the Point, and Mr. Peek is nowhere to be found!"

"Perhaps he has taken a telegraphic shock, too!"

"All the rest here?"

"Yes; but now, Captain Beckwith, you must be promoted to second groomsman."

Ignoring his objections in this latest emergency, I turned to Mrs. Painter, asking: "Will you give away the bride, thus standing for her mother?"

Equal to any emergency she replied: "We Friends do not understand thy services, but what will thee have me to do?"

"There is no time now to study up, but when the Pastor asks 'Who giveth this woman to be married to this man?' just step forward and say, 'I do'."

There was no danger of failure there. "Now wait until I run again to the chapel, to see if our minister is sufficiently coached, and then let the conquering victims come!"

The good man was ready, and quite delighted with the beautiful service. When we disagreed about the positions to be taken, he good-naturedly allowed himself to be backed against the rough little pulpit, and with an expression of amused curiosity prepared for the now waiting couple.

Perhaps a dozen camp friends had quietly entered and seated themselves to witness the ceremony, and all was ready. Hastily returning once more to our tent, and finding every one ready, and fearing that our little secret might be discovered, we ordered "Double quick." Bob and I went first together, the two groomsmen and bridesmaid entered from different directions. Sister Painter came next with the bride, and even in her well worn, patched brown 'every day', with travelling hat and pretty collar, she seemed quite beautiful. Hannah covered the retreat.

As we arranged our little wedding procession, the solemnity of the occasion became impressive, while the shades of evening struggled through the bare windows of the large chapel, and the gleam of half a dozen candles cast a glow over the Pastor's form as he stood, book in hand, awaiting the first sight of the twain, now slowly approaching. All fell, quietly and orderly, into position. And there, far from home and dear friends, in the roughly boarded, unplaned, unpainted structure where "the Boys in Blue" so often gathered to hear the words of love and truth, was solemnly performed the beautiful ceremony, without a pause or interruption, which joined two loving hearts as one in holy bonds, never to be severed on earth. "Whom God hath joined together, let no man put asunder."

More than one silent tear of thankfulness fell as the last prayer died away on the lips of the good man, who had so beautifully solemnized this institution.

Night had now fallen as all joyfully congratulated the noble looking, happy pair. They walked arm in arm, man and wife, back to our tents, where we quietly followed, no rumor having reached the alert ears of the poor weary fellows, anxious for a break in the monotony of hospital life.

The guests at the reception in our large tent consisted only of our own little party, and the refreshments were composed of a couple of bottles of Sister Painter's home-made wine, and a "wolverine" cake, hastily made by Mary Blackmar's willing hands.

Rev. —— wrote the certificate, and we had a merry time in witnessing it; while our tent was illuminated with two extra candles in bottles, and the wind made sweet music above our laughter on the swaying canvas roof. The great black log blazed brightly, now and then snapping out a sharp shout of joy, and all went merrily as the traditional marriage bell.

Bob, of course, was obliged to return at once to his

regiment; leaving his bride for a day or two while he cleaned up his regimental quarters, and obtained permission to go to housekeeping where bullets rained and shells stormed, and thither he took his happy bride.

About two weeks later came the furlough, and the Major's commission. On my return from my interview with Governor Fenton in Albany, I met the wedded pair in Washington, going North, where their festivities were continued among their friends with suitable formalities.

Chapter XX
New York State Agency

Quite unknown to me, the State Agents and the two Commissions had formulated an appeal to have me supersede Mrs. Spencer, then New York State Agent in the field, and urged that I go at once to Governor Fenton at Albany to have it confirmed. So the day after the wedding I started for New York on a government transport.

Mr. Houghton was also going North. The rumor of a wedding had already spread over camp, and Mr. Houghton and I were congratulated as the happy couple on our wedding trip. This caused a great deal of merriment.

Captain Blackman of the transport, was very kind and made the trip on the shabby boat quite pleasant. My little cabin was suffocating at night, and I left my door open with a light burning in the narrow passage-way, while the engineer and his wife slept opposite. Quite exhausted with preparations for the wedding and for my trip North, I fell into a heavy sleep. Some time during the night I was awakened by heavy hands passing up and down my body. I awoke in total darkness, and was too dazed at first to comprehend the situation, but at last I managed to exclaim "Who are you, and what do you want?"

A coarse voice, in broken English, said, "I want a place to sleep!"

I called for a light and help, when in a very calm manner the intruder said: "O, don't put yourself in a stew!" On his hastily retreating footsteps I quickly closed and locked the door. The engineer had doubtless extinguished the light in the passage before he closed their door.

The next day we stopped at Fortress Monroe, and were allowed to examine the interior of the Fort, and that great mounted black gun called "The Swamp Angel" which was reputed to throw a shot of four hundred pounds!

In Washington we met our old friend Major Baker; and when we walked up Pennsylvania Avenue toward the Capitol we saw the effect of an unusual freak of the wind. A large flag was flying at the top from either wing of the great building and both flags blew in towards each other, standing out immovable without a fold as if held by some material background. The effect was peculiar.

But I spent little time sight-seeing, and took the afternoon train for New York.

Upon arriving at my home in Bedford Avenue, Brooklyn, there were many matters to attend to, and I had little time to spend with my family. I then started for Albany. At Troy we crossed the river in a sleigh on thick ice. I had been invited to stop at the home of my former patient John C. Guffin, where I met his father, mother and brother. The parents reminded me of Abraham and Sarah. They seemed to have dropped out of the Old Testament, as they talked in Scripture language quite difficult for me to understand.

The hilly streets of Albany were covered with ice, and although a natural climber, I could not keep my footing, and so I simply sat down and slid to the bottom of those hills. Governor Fenton was away when I arrived, and I was obliged to remain three days waiting for him. During this time these hospitable patriarchs gave me, three times a day, only buckwheat cakes and tea, which peculiar diet caused a severe headache. I was very glad when I could get away. I never experienced such cold as during that visit.

Governor Fenton was very courteous, and, after examining the appeal made by all the State Agencies, the Sanitary and Christian Commissions, he soon granted the request and gave me the Commission of New York State agent, with directions to report to Mr. Morgan, head of New York State Agency in Washington.

On my return to Washington I met Mr. Morgan, and received from him the following commission:

"New York State Agency,
181 Pennsylvania Avenue,

Washington, D. C., February 22, 1865.
Colonel T. S. Bowers,
A. A. G. Armies, United States.

Sir:

Miss Ada W. Smith has been appointed agent of the State of New York for the relief of her soldiers.

I respectfully commend her to your kind consideration, assuring you that every facility given her for carrying out the object of her mission will be appreciated.

Very truly,
D. G. Morgan,
Supt. N. Y. S. Military Agency."

Mr. Morgan directed me to report to City Point and to relieve Mrs. Spencer.

On my return to City Point I met Major and Mrs. Eden. Having received his promotion and a furlough, they were on their wedding trip North. I was glad to return to City Point camp life and duty, with congratulations on all sides. The next day, with an ambulance and a friend, I went to Mrs. Spencer's quarters and showed her my commission, saying, "I would like to take possession in a few days."

Mrs. Spencer had been charged with partiality to McClellan men, and refusing Republican soldiers tobacco, etc. Politics, even in the army, caused many somersaults, and were quite beyond my management; and through some strategy my commission was revoked at City Point, though I retained the commission as New York agent in general!

There were then some indications of the collapse of the Confederacy, and that when this frightful war was over the agencies would also collapse. However, I kept on working in the old way, while my indignant Republican friends threatened, and tried to storm the New York State Agency. Politics ran high and many lost their heads politically. Many convalescent copperheads and Democrats, enlisted men, were allowed to go home to vote for president.

Doctor Painter, a strong Republican, incurred the displeasure of General Patrick, a Democrat, by some manipulations which enabled her to get enough passes for

Jersey soldiers to go home to vote and so balance the Democratic vote.

Many one-armed and one-legged men were moving about camp, waiting orders to report to Washington, where the Government would supply them with artificial limbs and discharge them. It was surprising how many were well fitted with these limbs, and that many could walk so well that only a slight limp betrayed them; while others with neatly gloved hands, which they could sometimes use quite well, were seldom observed in passing.

A young lieutenant from Maine, had lost a leg, and was lying, weary and helpless, on his hospital cot. He had written, as had many another poor fellow crippled for life, to his fiancée, offering to resign his claim, and he was now feverishly awaiting her reply. Day after day passed, and still no answer, while we tried every device to encourage him. He said "I know how it will be!" He became bitter and scornful and made no effort to live. While it was scarcely possible in any case that he could recover from this usually fatal thigh fracture, we still hoped that he might at least receive some word of comfort before he died.

I seldom went into the wards after nightfall, but the dying boy sent for me quite late one night. Hoping that some kind word had come at last, I hastened to his side. None had come and, conscious that his life was fast ebbing away, he had only bitterness for his former sweetheart and died with these cruel thoughts.

I wrote his friend, simply announcing his death; but a few days later came her reply, full of grief. She had received no letter, nor knew anything of his wounds. They had been friends from childhood and she could not believe she would never see him again. "Had he not mentioned her or left some word?" My reply was the saddest and most difficult of all sad letters, for—"It might have been." I tried to think of some word which he had dropped which might be happily construed, and I certainly strained a point to give this poor heart-stricken girl some little comfort to remember from the boy lover of her childhood.

A few days later his comrades carried him to a mournful tune of fife and drum, and fired a last salute over his lonely grave.

> "Of all sad words of tongue or pen,
> The saddest are these, it might have been."

CHAPTER XXI
A House Moving

General Collis, then in command of the colored brigade at the Point, on abandoning his adjutant's little frame house or office about fifteen feet by ten, kindly gave it to me. A large army wagon on which it was raised, for removal, supported by a squad of soldiers on either side, and hauled by six mules, made quite an impression coming up Agency Row, especially as it carried away the telegraph wires over the road. One of our large tents was moved to give it space, and the real door and little glass window in it made us quite the envy of the Row. It was divided into two rooms, having a tent roof. The front room was for business purposes. The smaller, which had a window about a foot square, was large enough only for a bunk with a straw bed, a packing box for a dresser, a hand glass and a barrel chair, and so New York was added to Pennsylvania and New Jersey Agencies.

This recalls a night incident somewhat later, when Mrs. Painter and I were sleeping in the bunk. I was startled by Mrs. Painter springing up on to the dresser and screaming loudly, "Murder! Thieves! Help!" almost in the face of a scamp at the window, who was evidently trying to reach the wines hidden under the dresser. Mrs. Painter was a very small woman of the old time Quaker stamp, and she wore a little white night cap, and the proverbial short gown and petticoat. As the poor fellow took to his heels and the neighbouring tents were aroused, I could only lie still and laugh at the ludicrous scene. He lost a great army shoe which rested conspicuously on a rise of ground, quite distant.

Another amusing incident comes to my mind in connection with my little house. One night there came a thundering knock on the door, on which remained the word

"Adjutant." On opening I found a soldier standing at attention and more than "half-seas-over," so that he could not distinguish a woman from an officer. He had been on furlough, and insisted on my taking his pass, but at last I succeeded in starting him for the proper office.

An incident occurs to me of a New York newspaper reporter who was invited to the mess of General Grant and staff. While drinking was more common than now, no one so far forgot himself as to become intoxicated in the presence of the General, whose self-control and rigid discipline all respected. But this man so demeaned himself as to "get under the table," and the officers present were excited to the utmost contempt and indignation at this breach of etiquette in the presence of the commander of the United States Armies. If intoxication had been common at Headquarters, camp gossip would certainly have travelled the half mile to the state agencies and brought us news of it. General Grant, however, was unhappily addicted to the excessive use of tobacco, which eventually caused him much suffering, and, later, his life.

Miss Jones, of Philadelphia

How few, even of the army veterans, remember the sacrifices of the "Women of the War" in hospitals, homes and elsewhere! In the many G. A. R. annual Memorial services held since the war, when they are received in churches to hear their heroic deeds extolled, never have I heard a chaplain or minister give a thought of the women workers, by whose faithful care many of these brave soldiers were nursed back to life, and restored to their anxious families and to the country.

Miss Jones, of Philadelphia, was one of these rare, forgotten workers. Accomplished, refined, though delicate, she left her luxurious home with its order and comforts, to give her time, strength and means to the principles of national liberty, inbred into the life of every citizen of Philadelphia by the frequent sight of the old cradle of the American flag, the little home of Betsey Ross, where, under the direction of General Washington, Lafayette and others—she sewed into the bunting the thirteen stars and stripes of our national emblem. A million subscribers, at ten cents each, have enabled the Association to make it a national or State reservation in the densest business section of the city, where it has become a national Mecca to thousands yearly visiting the City of Brotherly Love.

Miss Jones, on arriving at City Point Hospital, at once took up the rough camp life in an army tent with earth floor,—often damp and wet,—a little cot, an apology for a table, barrel chairs, the usual chimney built roughly of logs and mud with barrel top, the plain and sometimes distasteful food, and the atmosphere of the sick wards. Here, however, she worked for many weeks in that enthusiastic ardor which inspired her kindly heart, feeling that she was giving help, comfort, and perhaps life, to the sick who came under her care.

Thoughtless of self, and with failing strength, she continued to work ceaselessly, till, contracting typhoid fever, she collapsed quite suddenly, but still hoped that rest in the bare lonely tent might restore her to her hospital work.

I had been too much occupied with my sick Boys even to see Miss Jones, though much interested in her, having lived near her in Philadelphia some years before the war; and the sad news came with a shock that this frail, devoted soul had sacrificed her life to her country and died in the field, like many a true soldier and patriot, far from friends and the home where every tender luxury was awaiting her.

Doctor Painter and I volunteered to sit beside her slight form during the night, which was intensely cold, while a full moon shed its silvery rays over the phantom of midnight silence in camp, and glittered like rare crystals on the pure white snow that seemed to reach the distant horizon, whence the brilliant stars looked down in love and pity. Mrs. Painter and I sat on rough chairs with our feet on logs, while the fire logs in the crude chimney burned brightly. Mrs. Painter, who had been among the first women to reach the front, meanwhile told me many a tale of her strange experiences when system had not reached the improvised temporary hospital tents, where many suffered for help and nourishment then unattainable. So the night passed, while the moaning wind sang "Rest, sweet soul," often slightly swaying the white sheet that covered the pallid body. More than once we started quickly to the seeming motion of life, hoping it might be real, but the pure spirit had passed on, while the frail body rested with a pleasant smile, calmly, as if tended by the friends of home and the formalities of a last funeral service for the dead.

Her brother, Horatio, came for the body, and at last it was laid away among her ancestors in the family lot near Philadelphia.

Recognition of her services has been given in Philadelphia by the naming of one of the G. A. R. Posts "the Hetty Jones Post."

The only other post that I have ever heard of named after a woman is the Betsey Ross Post, also of Philadelphia.

From Harper's Weekly
Saturday April 30th, 1864
(By Private Miles O'Reilly)
Gen. Chas. Halpin.

> Three years ago to-day
> We raised our hands to heaven,
> And on the rolls of muster
> Our names were thirty-seven;
> There were just a thousand bayonets,
> And the swords were thirty-seven,
> As we took the oath of service
> With our right hands raised to heaven.
> Oh, 'twas a gallant day,
> In memory still adored,
> That day of our sun-bright nuptials
> With the musket and the sword!
> Shrill rang the fifes, the bugles blared,
> And beneath a cloudless heaven
> Twinkled a thousand bayonets,
> And the swords were thirty-seven.
> Of the thousand stalwart bayonets
> Two hundred march to-day;
> Hundreds lie in Virginia swamps,
> And hundreds in Maryland clay;

And other hundreds, less happy, drag
Their shattered limbs around,
And envy the deep, long, blessed sleep
Of the battle-field's holy ground.
For the swords—one night, a week ago,
The remnant, just eleven,
Gathered around a banqueting board
With seats for thirty-seven;
There were two limped in on crutches,
And two had each but a hand
To pour the wine and raise the cup
As we toasted "Our flag and land!"
And the room seemed filled with whispers
As we looked at the vacant seats,
And, with choking throats, we pushed aside
The rich but untasted meats;
Then in silence we brimmed our glasses,
As we rose up—just eleven,
And bowed as we drank to the loved and the dead
Who had made us thirty-seven!

Chapter XXII
The Last Parade of Confederate Prisoners

"I am quite confident that Love was the only rope thrown out to us by Heaven when we fell overboard into life."— Sidney Lanier.[2]

General Grant had ordered a grand attack all along the lines from Appomattox to Hatches Run. This was the fateful move that crushed the Confederate Army, and opened the way to Petersburg and Richmond on April 3d.

The paroled and surrendered Confederate prisoners were at once marched forward from Petersburg on the road beside the hospital. It was a strange, sad sight, this long line of Confederate prisoners, 3,000 strong, officers and men without arms,— some by habit reaching for the forfeited sword, belt, or gun,— worn, tired, begrimed figures of despair. They were clothed in every degree of shabbiness, from the dulled tinsel of the uniformed officers, to the worn, faded, ragged grey that they had so confidently donned at the beginning of the war. They were on their way to City Point under guard, many to be forwarded to some Northern camp, where at least their starving bodies would be fed and made comfortable.

---

[2] Sidney Lanier, later musician, poet, writer, on the secession of Georgia at once enlisted in the Confederate infantry and served through the war except while a prisoner at Point Lookout. He afterwards rejoiced in the overthrow of slavery; and knew that it was belief in the soundness and greatness of the American Union, among the millions of the North and the great North West that really conquered the South. He said "As soon as Lee invaded the North and arrayed the sentiment against us our swift destruction followed."— Edward Mims.

There was no sound of exultation over the conquered enemy among the Northern men and women standing quietly near to see them pass. Some even saluted the defeated Confederate officers. None showed the slightest disrespect to those unfortunates who had not only lost, in a futile war against their own nation, the "Flower of their Chivalry," but their broad acres were devastated and had become battle fields of frightful carnage and struggle, and their homes were also wrecked, leaving many without shelter, and thus depriving hundreds of any present means of support. As they marched slowly by, in painful silent dejection, did they realize the folly of an ill-advised rebellion, to which they had sacrificed lives, homes and sustenance to an illogical, unethical romantic ideal?

Crowds of barefoot, ragged negroes, nearly nude, who had been shut up for years in Petersburg, now crowded by hundreds along the road. One excited old woman, her head covered with a faded bandana, exclaimed: "Lor, dere goes ole Mars, I knows him shore. Can't tech me now. I'se a free nigger." Another shouted to us, "I knows you alls Yankee ladies, de Lord bress you."

It seemed like a funeral procession, without fife and drum, as it wound slowly past the hospital to City Point United States Headquarters, there to take their parole.

About this time, at City Point, I saw General Custer, who lost his life soon after in the Indian raids. He was a small, spare, nervous man, wearing a scarlet-lined cape thrown over his shoulder, and his long light hair floated back, making a striking picture of a cavalryman as his spirited horse dashed from one headquarters to another.

CHAPTER XXIII
Our First Sight of Petersburg

The advance on Petersburg occurred on April 2d, 1865. It was about 3.30 A. M. when our troops entered the city, and all were anxious to see the city so long besieged and coveted.

Two days later, on the 4th, a party of about twenty-five officers and ladies of the hospital, some well mounted, some in ambulances, started in high exultation for the conquered city. I was happy in being mounted on a beautiful white horse, with a crimson saddle cloth, loaned from United States Headquarters. I wore a dark blue habit with infantry buttons, a fatigue cap with chin strap, riding gloves, and carried a small whip. The horse acted as if trained for a circus, full of antics as a pet dog. In defiance of rein and whip he walked on every stray log, into ditches, or puddles of water in the road, first raising his haunches to feel if I were firm in the saddle, and travelled with a "lope" as easy as a rocking chair, so that after twenty-five miles I was not in the least tired.

We rode over the fields of the last skirmish, torn ground, destroyed entrenchments, the "Cheveaux de frieze," broken and scattered among clothing, canteens and the general debris of a battle-field. At the outskirts of the city we saw great "gopher holes" dug in the sides of hills, where the inhabitants crowded daily to escape the shells that were constantly falling into the doomed city. In these holes they were safe until nightfall, when firing usually ceased and the weary women and children returned to their homes to sleep until another day. Shots passed through many houses but it was surprising that so little had been destroyed.

GENERAL O. B. WILCOX

Having previously met General O. B. Wilcox, who was then in command of the city, we rode to his headquarters, where I introduced our party. He received us courteously, giving us a mounted escort, that no trouble might ensue while we made a tour of the almost deserted city. The windows were all closed, as for some national mourning. There was only one foolish demonstration, by some young women on a piazza, who made grimaces at our handsome officers, and gyrated their fingers at them in a most remarkable manner. I was sorry and indignant for this petty spite, but our brave men merely smiled without comment.

The houses were generally detached, small and shabby, showing little to interest beside occasional marks made by stray shot. While riding through the town we saw an old gentleman weeding his garden, and I made the excuse of asking for a glass of water, which was politely given. I said to him, "You appear to be taking things very quietly."

In his strong Southern accent, he replied: "Oh yes; you uns have us beaten, and we might as well make the best of it and go to work."

During this memorable day in Petersburg we had visited our old friend Bob Eden, who became editor of the Petersburg Progress, a Confederate paper, immediately after the occupation of the city; and he, like his comrades, was wild with joy at the turn of things, political and national.

The following from "Grant's" Petersburg Progress appeared the day after our visit. The paper is still in my possession, but it has nearly fallen in pieces. There was no supply of printer's blank paper, and the Confederates had been obliged to use one side of wall paper, or anything else that would hold print.

"Grant's Petersburg Progress,
Petersburg, Va., 1865, April 4th.
    Vol. 1, No. 2

Proprietors: Major R. C. Eden, Captain C. H. McCreary.
Eternal vigilance is the price of peace, (and ten cents for our paper.)"

I copy from one column the following significant advertisements:

"NOTICE"
"All persons destitute of provision will apply as follows: In West Ward, to W. L. Lancaster, East Ward, to W. L. Lancaster, Central Ward, to W. L. Lancaster, South Ward, to W. L. Lancaster."

Surely there was little animosity when our troops cheerfully offered food and sustenance to the destitute, starving whites, as well as to the helpless negroes.

"AUCTION SALES"
"To be sold cheap (if not badly sold already) all that singularly ineligible worthless property, known as the Southern Confederacy; for particulars apply to Jefferson Davis. N. B. Liberal terms to agents of Maximilian, Louis Napoleon or Victoria."

In this same crude issue appears the following, probably the last notice of a sale of slaves that ever disgraced our nominally free country; now happily the home of freedom in very truth, though so long permitting, in the face of our boasted freedom, the sale of human beings.

"I will sell to the highest bidder, for cash, at Notoway Court House, on Thursday, the sixth day of April, next Court day, ten negroes belonging to the estate of Uriah Lipscomb, deceased.

P. A. Lipscomb,
Com. Co. Court Notoway."

"Editorial Comment— The above sale is postponed indefinitely; a different disposition of the property having been made by Mr. A. Lincoln, of the White House, Washington, D. C."

"Lady visitors: Our sanctum was yesterday graced by several ladies, and all of them loyal and of strong Union principles. The party composed of Miss H. P. (high private) Smith, Agent from New York State, Mrs. Colonel Logan, Mrs. Sample, Delaware Agent, and Mrs. Huron, Indiana Agent. Their presence was very acceptable, and did much to soothe and comfort us in our labor. They were under escort of Messers. Clark, Peek and Brown, of the Sanitary Commission."

"THE TWO MINNIES"
By A Rebel Soldier
(Suggested by a letter from Minnie, saying that she prayed daily that the "Minnie" balls might spare me.)

"There is a Minnie that I love,

And a "Minnie" that I fear,
But the former is now absent,
And the latter oft too near.
But the Minnie prays for me each day
That to "Minnie" I'll not fall a prey.
"The voice of one is soft and sweet
The other harsh and shrill—
One only speaks to bless mankind
The other but to kill.
And while Minnie prays for me each day
Yankee "Minnie" seek me for a prey.
"And when this sad war is over,
Our independence won,
I'll bid adieu to Yankee "Minn"
And seek the other one.
And together render thanks each day
That to Yankee "Minns" I never fell a prey."

To see the victorious veterans of the Army returning and marching through Petersburg was a never-to-be-forgotten sight. As we sat, mounted, at the corner of a street, they marched by with easy swinging tramp, by hundreds and thousands, dust-begrimed, in faded threadbare blue uniforms that they had worn through many a bloody battle, and in which they had slept many nights, often in swamps, and mud on the battle-fields. The shabby knapsacks, battered canteens, ragged blankets, their well-polished old guns, the only fresh clean emblem in sight; and these for the most part were shouldered as if for a holiday, which in very truth it was, probably the happiest they ever enjoyed. Discipline of the tired host was quite forgotten, while the worn, faded, torn flags floated out proudly.

The Eighth Wisconsin Infantry had some time before sent home their mascot "Old Abe," the hero of twenty battles and many skirmishes. This eagle was taken from its nest by an Indian and presented to Company C., where it became the pet of the regiment. During attacks he was carried at the front on a standard, near the flag,—sometimes held by a long cord or chain,—he would rise up flapping his great wings, and screeching defiance at the enemy loudly enough to be heard along the line. His reputation made thousands of dollars at fairs and elsewhere. His portrait was painted, and hangs in the Old South Church, Boston. The State pensioned Old Abe and supported an attendant to care for him. He died at last of old age, and his skin is stuffed and safely preserved in the state archives at Madison, Wisconsin.

As these men tramped to the music of the shrill fife and drum, that knew no rest that day, they sometimes joined in a great chorus, meanwhile cheering themselves hoarse, to the tunes of "Johnny Came Marching Home," "Yankee Doodle," and many an army song.

When some former patients recognized us, surgeons and nurses who had cared for them, they broke all bounds, and, with uncovered heads, dipped their tattered flags and fairly roared their thanks in grateful cheers, while we waved our caps and handkerchiefs in return and also cheered. The magnetism of a home-going victorious army spread like a prairie fire, not only from regiment to regiment, but extended to every individual in their presence, while a roar as if of ocean waves spread over the sea of happy men and women.

This was a day of great rejoicing and enthusiasm among soldiers and Northerners, never to be forgotten. Taking leave of our polite escort, and thanking General Wilcox for his kindness, the mounted party took a spirited gallop back to hospital camp.

Strict hospital discipline was relaxed and the men were singing "Home, Sweet Home," "Yankee Doodle," "John Brown's Body," "Marching Through Georgia," and many other patriotic songs, enjoying them equally, until taps ordered "Lights out," when the whole camp soon fell into peaceful dreams of home.

TAPS

"Night draws her sable mantle on
And pins it with a star."
Darkness has come, and rest is won
By those who thro' the dusty way,
Have marched their long and weary day.
And now the bugler from his tent
Across the prairies far,

Comes forth to blow the call.
By him 'tis sent. The regiment
Will hear and know the hour has come
For sleep, until the rising sun
Shall summon one and all.
Lights out! Lights out! The bugle's clear
Notes falling on the air,
Sound to the ear now far, now near;
Now almost ceasing, now enhanced
By echoes o'er that wide expanse
Of prairies bleak and bare.
Lights out! Lights out! From every lamp
The light is seen to die.
With measured tramp around the camp
The sentries guard against their foes;
The rest are wrapped in sweet repose
Beneath the starry sky.
"Taps" falls far sweeter on the air
Than any other sound.
Like opiate rare, it soothes all care—
To weary men a blessing seems—
And pleasant are the soldier's dreams
Tho' stretched upon the ground.
Ah, Taps, thy mournful signal call
Floats o'er a new-made grave,
Thy soft notes fall where one from all
Life's weary march forever rests—
Asleep. Where wild birds build their nests,
Unmindful of the brave.

John P. Force.

There were yet many patients, so that our work at the hospital went on as before, while waiting for further orders; while all soon became conscious of a general relaxation of the imperative discipline that had made our hospital a model of general courtesy, neatness, and order.

Chapter XXIV
Preparing for a Visit to Richmond, the Capital of the Lost Confederacy

"In giving freedom to the slave we assure freedom to the free."—Abraham Lincoln.

A few days after the evacuation and capture of Richmond, a small party led by Mr. J. Yates Peek, of Brooklyn, still superintendent of the Sanitary Commission at City Point, arranged to make an early start on the morning of April 11th, to see the smoking city. Everything must be arranged overnight, and I planned so as to jump quickly into my clothing, placing my only pair of good boots on a near-by chair, to lose no time. But in the morning, almost at the last moment, the boots were missing. When all had joined in the search, to no effect, the mystery increased.

We had a boy orderly, named Jack, who was more officious than useful, and often much in the way, and he volunteered in the search. Returning to my little room after a moment's absence, to my astonishment I beheld the boy on the floor with his head in my trunk, which he had had the temerity to unlock. He was rummaging and disarranging everything as if with a pudding stick. I exclaimed: "Jack, what are you doing?" in no pleasant tone of voice.

"I thought the shoes might be in the trunk," he quite coolly replied, "but I've been through every darned thing in it and they ain't there."

Words were, at that hurried moment, quite inadequate. An explanation of the loss of the shoes came later. We had removed a small stove and left the pipe hole open on the side between two tents, and during the night some ambitious contraband probably had squeezed into the small space between the tents, and with a long stick had "gobbled" my only pair of decent shoes.

What could I do? I must go somewhere, as the party were not willing to go without me. Fortunately, Miss Dupee, assistant in the Maine State Agency, had a pair which fitted quite well and she very kindly loaned them to me. One of the pleasant associations of agency life in camp was the camaraderie that made all things in common, just as the soldier shared his last ration or his last dollar with another comrade in the field.

Owing to this delay, we were barely able to catch the boat as it was pushing off at City Point Dock. A pleasant sail on the James River brought us to the dock of the Seven-Hilled City, directly into the burned and still smoking district.

The fleeing citizens in their short-sighted frenzy, had determined to destroy the whole city. But thanks to the efforts of the Federal soldiers, chiefly colored, the greater part of the city was saved for them, while the factories and warehouses continued to smoke and burn for many weeks.

It was this same obstructed wharf and destroyed dock over which the President climbed, holding little Tad by the hand. They passed through the burned district, against the protest of a small escort, while jostled by a rough crowd.

Blessed by the grateful negroes crowding around the great Emancipator, some kneeling and kissing the hem of his coat, he strode fearlessly on among enemies and friends.

A significant fact to be forever cherished by the freed race is that General Weitzel, with the 25th Corps d' Afric, took possession of the conquered city; and further that a colored soldier carried the President's United States flag before him into the heart of Richmond, where it was raised over the Capitol, and Richmond was once more and forever in the Union.

The Capitol, a modest building with white columns and dome, was uninjured. There were many comfortable-looking detached houses, with yards or gardens pleasant to see after the bare tent life at City Point Hospital.

We dined at Spotswood Hotel, still managed by a Confederate host, where we greatly enjoyed fresh peas and corn. We were rather disappointed by the plainness of the gray mastic front of the three-storied double medium house of Jefferson Davis, both inside and out, with only a door yard in front, where I gathered some leaves which are still in my possession.

We saw the entrance to the tunnel that was dug by starving, desperate Yankee prisoners, almost in full view of the guards, quite near Libby prison, and by which many had escaped to freedom, thus bringing more deprivation and abuse upon the despairing prisoners left behind.

All was now changed in the city. The inhabitants finding they were not pursued or in any way molested, were gradually returning to their homes and buildings that they had not succeeded in destroying.

LIBBY PRISON

Libby Prison remained; a weather-stained brick tobacco storehouse, the former scene of so much suffering and indignity. But the tables were now turned. The brutal turnkey, Captain Richard Turner, by name, I think, was now himself a prisoner. He was a stocky, brutal-looking fellow. All people were allowed to pass and look through a small open window at the miserable wretch, while he defiantly mounted a stool in the middle of the room to show himself more conspicuously. That morning a former prisoner had cajoled him into coming close to the small window, where the man struck through and felled him to the ground as he said: "Take that for the pail of filth you threw over me while I was a helpless prisoner."

GENERAL ULYSSES GRANT

It was a fine commentary upon the discipline and

forbearance of many liberated victims, that they did not kill or shoot this monster for his atrocities, instead of merely gazing and glaring at him silently through the small opening.

GENERAL LEE

PEACE

When the formal announcement of the final surrender of General Lee to General Grant, at Appomattox, on the 9th of April, 1865, was confirmed in the camp, all knew that at last the "cruel war" was over. There was great rejoicing in the hospital, and all began to prepare to go North, or home again, after so many weary years of struggle. Some wept for joy as they wrote to the weary waiting watchers at home; some were to carry to their friends and neighbors the last words and deeds of the many who slept beneath the soil of Virginia, or further south, while their comrades "went marching on." The workers of the Agencies and the Commissions had so long labored in the same spirit that we were much like a large united family; and until we departed one by one for our homes, we did not realize how close was the bond of sympathy and affection, that could never be forgotten.

CHAPTER XXV
Recollections of Lincoln

"We are not enemies, but friends. We must not be enemies. Though passion may have strained, it must not break our bonds of affection. The mystic chords of memory stretching from every battlefield and patriot grave to every living heart and hearthstone, all over this broad land, will yet swell the chorus of the Union, when again touched, as surely they will be by the better angels of our nature."—Abraham Lincoln.

During the last year of the war I was still working for the "Boys" at City Point Depot Field Hospital, Virginia, half a mile from the headquarters of the United States Armies in the field, at the junction of the Appomattox and James Rivers, when the day of the second inaugural drew near. This caused a welcome ripple of excitement to spread over the daily monotony of discipline in hospital camp life. The fearless President was to stand once more before the people to take the oath to uphold the institutions and principles of his country, despite the state policy as well as humanity that had compelled the passing of the Emancipation Act, that had cut the last thread of hope for the return of "the good old days" of the South.

When Abraham Lincoln, with superhuman courage, made that moral stroke of the pen that gave freedom to millions of slaves, then was born at last a free country, not only in name, but in the glorious fact that had blotted out from our country's escutcheon the shame of human slavery that had so long branded our vaunted freedom as a disgrace. The people, the great middle class, the saviours of freedom who in great crises rise to a national emergency like a towering Gibraltar, had risen to uphold the weary hands of him who loved his country more than life, though so often it had seemed as if the waves of care and sorrow would engulf his tired soul.

ABRAHAM LINCOLN

Many officers, and others able to secure leave of absence or passes, hastened to witness this greatest of our national events. With other State Agency ladies, I was anxious to break the long strain of caring for sick and wounded patients amid scenes of the horrors of war and bloodshed. Nine thousand men, at different times, filled this well-organized camp. Mangled bodies were brought directly in from the battle-fields where they had fallen, by means of temporary rails, on rough bare sand cars, on which they were piled like so many logs, one upon another, so great was the need of haste to get them to the hospital. All of these were covered with dirt, powder, blood, torn uniforms, and seemed an almost indistinguishable mass; while many a half-severed limb dangled from a shattered human trunk.

I was fortunate in being able to go to Washington quite independently, without fear of detention, having a pass from General Grant that ordered all guards, pickets, steamboats and government roads to pass "Miss Ada W. Smith," and which practically would have allowed me to travel free without question over the entire Northern States, as all roads were then under government control. Thus was I enabled to accept the invitation of Dr. Hettie K. Painter, Pennsylvania State Agent, and her husband, to join their party going to Washington. On arriving in that city we went to a small hotel, where we met some Western friends, and found there also a former patient from City Point, Lieutenant Gosper, who had lost a leg in the skirmish before Petersburg, and was now convalescent. He manifested the usual cheerfulness of wounded men, while waiting to have an artificial limb adjusted,—a free gift from the government.

We had secured tickets and good places to see the official ceremony; but the surging mass of humanity crowded us quite beyond hearing. On this eventful morning a raw, threatening gale blew dust and loose debris into our eyes and faces, nearly blinding us.

"And men looked up with mad disquietude upon the dull sky," as we awaited the signal of the President's coming. At last the tall, gaunt form of Mr. Lincoln came forward on to the portico of the Capitol, surrounded by officials and attendants. Chief Justice Chase opened the great Bible, and President Lincoln stepped forward, placing his hand upon the book to take, for the second time, his oath of office. At this moment, the leaden sky, that had not lifted during the day, suddenly opened a small rift, while a strong bright ray of sunshine shot through and rested upon the noble head of the soon-to-be-glorified martyr. A silence of awe seemed for a moment to overspread the startled multitude, and then the darkening gloom closed down again as with an ominous foreboding. But not a word of that memorable address could we hear above the soughing, cold, gusty wind.

While planning for the reception, our young lieutenant, sensitive and refined, positively declined to accompany us, repeating only: "It is no place for a cripple."

After we had exhausted all other arguments, a happy thought came to me: "Well, Lieutenant, if you will not go with us I suppose I shall have to stay away also; each of the other ladies has an escort, and, as every lady must be attended, I can not go alone."

"Would you go to a reception with a cripple on a crutch?" he replied, sadly.

My answer came quickly and sincerely: "I would be proud of such an escort!"

At last he consented, rather reluctantly, to accompany us. At the appointed hour we started for the evening reception. Soon, however, we found ourselves in a frightful crush of people, crowding up the White House steps, and we quickly closed around the lieutenant, fearing he might get under foot. Our party was carried up bodily to the landing, where I found that my arm was quite badly bruised by the crutch.

After getting breath and composing ourselves, we fell into the long procession of couples approaching the President, where the ushers went through the form of taking our names and introducing us. In passing we saw a group of cabinet officers and a number of ladies with Mrs. Lincoln, who was gowned in white satin with a deep black thread lace flounce over an expansive skirt, in the style of that day; and she wore her favorite head dress, a wreath of natural pink roses entirely around her plainly dressed hair.

The President's band played stirring airs in an adjoining room, while crowds of every grade passed on, some in dashing uniforms, some in evidently fresh "store clothes," others in gorgeous costumes, and the good women from the country in sensible black,—with ill-fitting gloves. It was a motley democratic crowd, such as could be seen in no royal country, and of which we are justly proud. Following the almost endless procession we saw the unmistakable form of Mr. Lincoln, his long arm and white-gloved hand reaching out to shake hands, and bowing in a mechanical manner, plainly showing that he wished this demand of the people was well over.

Suddenly straightening up his tall form, while continuing the handshaking, he looked eagerly down the line and, to my surprise, as the lieutenant and I approached, he stepped out before us and, grasping the hand of the crippled soldier, he said in an unforgettable tone of deep sympathy: "God bless you, my boy! God bless you!" Owing to the lieutenant's crutch I was obliged to take his left arm which brought me on the outside away from the President. I attempted to pass with a bow, but he stood in my way, still holding out his large hand, until I released mine and gave it to him, receiving a warm, sympathetic grasp. Then I saw that wonderful lighting of his kindly beneficent grey eyes, that for a moment often beautified as with a halo that otherwise plain, sad face. As we moved on, the lieutenant exclaimed in happy exultation, "Oh! I'd lose another leg for a man like that!"

Such was the magnetic tone and touch of that rare spirit that carried hope and trust to the hopeless sorrowing, the great heart that could with truth and sincerity enfold not only his own country, but the whole human brotherhood of the world, and caused him to reply in effect to those who wished him to subscribe to some special creed: "When I can find a church broad enough to take in the whole human race, then I will join it."

Once again I saw President Lincoln, after the inaugural, early in April—that fateful month in which occurred the last battle of the rebellion, the surrender of heroic Lee, the act of the magnanimous Grant, the imprisonment of the Confederate leader, the conference of those great men of war and state.

When Abraham Lincoln had come, in his own boat the River Queen, to meet Grant and Sherman at City Point, he was so secure in the conclusion of peace at last, that he had brought Mrs. Lincoln and "little Tad" to share in the general rejoicing.

I did not see Mrs. Lincoln at that time, and I had also missed seeing her in 1863, when I had taken to the famous Soldier's Rest and Hospital in Philadelphia one soldier blinded by a bullet that passed through his head, cutting both optic nerves, one who had lost both legs, and another who had lost both arms.

During the war, when the troops were en route to the front and halted in Philadelphia, the great Liberty Bell announced their coming, and hundreds of women and many men hastened with bountiful supplies to this great Rest, where they set up rough wooden tables. Here many passing regiments had a generous meal, and almost lifted the roof with their grateful shouts, exceeded only by those of the outside crowd as they marched away to the jolly tune of the fife and drum.

At City Point the three Titans of war and state—Lincoln, Grant and Sherman—met with navy and state officers to conclude the terms of surrender and peace. There was no desire to confirm the battle cry, "Hang Jeff Davis," as in most countries would have been inevitable, and even sympathy and mercy inspired the closing acts of this national tragedy that had cost the lives of thousands of brave Southerners, and of those of the invincible North.

During this mighty conclave at City Point, Abraham Lincoln was occasionally seen riding to the front and about camp and hospital, and to visit the tents, in his sombre black suit and high hat towering above many striking uniforms about him. It was a singular fact that while many ministers had come down to "overlook the field" dressed in the same fashion, except that there was always somehow a ministerial dip of the front corners of their long frock coats that at once betrayed their profession, they were often ridiculed and guyed by the rough soldiers. Yet the thought of ridicule was never suggested for this unique man who seemed to dignify and honor everything he touched, even when, in the same style, he rode his horse in an ungainly manner. He could have ridden bareback without loss of dignity.

On one of these occasions Mr. Lincoln had ridden up from the Point to visit our hospital, and was, as usual, accompanied by crowds of devoted friends as he walked through the divisions and avenues of the different camps. There were gathered the sick and wounded of the Ninth, Sixth, Fifth, Second Corps, and the Corps d' Afric, who were frequently visited by their regimental surgeons and officers of regiments that were encamped before Petersburg.

I shall always regret not speaking to Mr. Lincoln at that time. It would have been very easy to do, but I could not see the coming catastrophe, and I hesitated to push forward into the surrounding crowd to be presented. As he passed from tent to tent, with many a cheerful word to the suffering men, a young man connected with the Sanitary Commission, now Doctor Jerome Walker, a successful physician of Brooklyn, said, pointing to some tents near-by, "Mr. President, you do not want to go in there!"

"Why not, my boy?" he asked.

"Why, sir, they are sick rebel prisoners."

With a hasty movement he said, "That is just where I do want to go," and he strode within the tent, shaking hands and speaking such words of comfort as only his magnanimous spirit could prompt, to the grateful surprise and pleasure of the Confederate patients.

ANNOUNCEMENT OF THE
DEATH OF PRESIDENT LINCOLN

On the morning of April 15th, 1865, as the sun rose over our quiet hospital camp, I was startled by the sound of galloping hoofs, that stopped suddenly before our tent. Scratching on the canvas indicated the usual sign for admission. Hastily untying the tent flaps, I found Major William Baker, of the Tenth Colored Troops, still mounted, and betraying much agitation and haste, when he said: "I have just ridden up to tell you, the first person in the hospital, the sad news of the reported death of the President. All officers were assembled at 2 A. M. to a conference, when the reported assassination by Wilkes Booth was read, but not yet officially confirmed." With a sad expression and a salute he put spurs to his horse and dashed back to City Point.

Telegrams were slow in those days, so it was not till the afternoon that the terrible, cruel tragedy was announced at the hospital camp. The shock was paralyzing, and a sombre silence spread over the wards containing the men who had learned to love this great soul. Men and women as well as soldiers wept together as for a loved, indulgent father, who had borne his crushing responsibilities without a murmur or a cry for help. A few copperhead patients dared to approve of the murderous act, but they were soon beaten into silence with the crutches of the indignant crippled convalescents.

MAJOR WILLIAM BAKER

J. WILKES BOOTH

With a vague desire to express in some way their grief, men came and begged for a bit of black to fasten over their tents, and if any were so luckless as to have a black suit they saw it speedily reduced to shreds and flying from the entrances of the wards or tents. But other men still begged so earnestly for some black emblem, that I at last gave to them a full train black skirt that I could illy spare. This soon became floating ribbons over many a tent, to the great satisfaction of the loyal boys, having so little by which they could express their sorrow. In a few days some of us were so fortunate as to receive from home or from Washington, mourning badges of suitable designs, which we wore as a mark of respect to our dead President.

In making the rounds among my scattered patients I stopped to speak to Major Prentiss, of a New York regiment, who had captured his wayward young brother—a Captain in the Sixth Maryland Confederate Infantry—now lying in the same ward quite near, having lost a leg. The Captain, a handsome, cheerful youth, whose happy jokes and stories kept his neighbours quite diverted from the tedium of convalescence, was recovering slowly; but the Major had been shot through the lung, and one could hear the air passing through the unhealed wound. He looked so longingly at the badge I was wearing, that another brother, who had come South to take the patients home if possible, said: "He would be so happy if he could have a badge." It was impossible to ignore the wish of a dying soldier, so I took off the one I was wearing and pinned it over his heart. He could not speak his thanks, but a rare smile of intense satisfaction spread over the sufferer's countenance.

As in most great catastrophes, it seemed for a time as if the world must stand still; but many patients still needed care, and we were obliged to go on with our work till all the sick were sent home or to Northern hospitals, and each resumed his daily duty, while the spirit of sadness hovered over the hospital campus.

Lincoln was not a type,
No ancestors, no fellows, no successors.
Ingersoll.

O CAPTAIN! MY CAPTAIN!

O Captain! my Captain! our fearful trip is done,
The ship has weathered every rack, the prize we sought
    is won,
The port is near, the bells I hear, the people all exulting,
While follow eyes the steady keel, the vessel grim and
    daring;
But O heart! heart! heart!

O the bleeding drops of red,
Where on the deck my Captain lies,
Fallen cold and dead.
O Captain! my Captain! rise up and hear the bells;
Rise up—for you the flag is flung—for you the bugle
    trills,
For you bouquets and ribboned wreaths—for you the
    shores a-crowding,
For you they call, the swaying mass, their eager faces
    turning;
Here Captain! dear father!
This arm beneath your head!
It is some dream that on the deck
You've fallen cold and dead.
My Captain does not answer, his lips are pale and still,
My father does not feel my arm, he has no pulse nor will,
The ship is anchored safe and sound, its voyage closed
    and done,
From fearful trip the victor ship comes in with object
    won;
Exult O shores, and ring O bells
But I, with mournful tread,
Walk the deck, my Captain lies,
Fallen cold and dead.

Walt Whitman.

CHAPTER XXVI

A Recent Letter from Doctor Mary Blackmar Bruson

"Jacksonville, Florida,
April, 1910.

My Dear Ada:

At your request I send some incidents of camp life as they come to mind.

After one of the fearful onslaughts at Petersburg, the wounded came pouring into my tent, which was nearest to the firing line, so that a drummer-lad had named it 'The Half Way House'. One lad dropped from the wagon in which he was being transported, as they passed my tent. I ran and cried out to the driver. He coolly replied 'He is dead, what does it matter!'

I knelt by the boy's side and found a remote evidence of life, but hemorrhage was so profuse it seemed he could not survive. I called the attention of surgeons, but all said 'We must go on'. So with my knowledge that life was not extinct, and that he was so young and had the force of youth, (moreover the hardships of the Confederates had toughened him), I remained on the ground at his side not daring to leave him, but compelled to use my fingers as a tampon.

I remained with him twenty-four hours before I felt safe in having him carried to a ward. Cramped and exhausted from such a strain, in addition to weakness induced by loss of sleep through nights and days previous, I could hardly crawl into my tent. Being cold I heated a brick, put it in my cot and was soon so deeply sunk in oblivion, it seemed I would have remained so forever, but for my companions, Misses V. and M., who came in at midnight. Soon after they retired they discovered a dense smoke filling the tent and were aware of burning wool. They called me again and again, but getting no reply they jumped up and pulled me from the burning cot and finally roused me, so that I calmly dressed.

Morning found my limbs, from ankles to knees, one solid blister, but this I was at first too stupid to realize, or even the danger which I had escaped through my faithful friends. No one knew of the accident but ourselves, and I went about my work as usual. Nature alone was the healer.

One day I asked a poor exhausted soldier—so feeble from disease and exposure that he could only whisper—if there was anything he wished, and said that if so I would try to get it for him. With tears and sighs he replied, "O, Miss, if you would only get me some fried bacon with molasses poured over it, I would get well!" It was a novel dish to me but was easily attained, and the man's appetite was so quickened by the relishable food that he began to recover forthwith. In later years I learned that very many looked upon it as a special delicacy.

I was finally placed in charge of the Confederate wards, and there saw that grandest of men, President Lincoln. This was after the last assault on Petersburg, and men horribly wounded and sick, from both armies, were rushed into our camp hospital at City Point. I was given especial care of the private Confederates, and my companion, that fine, grand woman, Miss Vance, took charge of the Confederate officers. I had only an orderly to assist me—a boy about sixteen,—and what with the cleaning and caring for each sick, torn body, our powers were strained to the utmost limit of endurance. Our patients' cots were so close together that we could just squeeze between, and our ward so long that it required from three to four tents.

General Grant was at City Point, and President Lincoln came down at this time, before our army marched into Richmond. One day both of them were coming slowly down my avenue. The orderly rushed in and cried out—'President Lincoln's coming!' I was at the extreme end of the hospital tent, but, girl-like, started forward that I might see him. At that instant, oh, such a puny, helpless wail, as of sick and dying infants, issued from every throat: 'Oh, don't leave us, Miss! He is a beast! He will kill us!'

I replied: 'Oh, no! He is a grand good man!' Again and again came forth that puny wail, 'Don't leave us, Miss!' till I finally said, 'Well, I'll not leave you, don't fear!' but by that time I had got to the front of the tent and the orderly had pulled back a flap on my request so that I peered out. Within about fifteen or twenty feet were both men. General Grant with the inevitable cigar, and President Lincoln, so tall, so lank, giving evidence of much sorrow, looming over him. I heard General Grant say distinctly, 'These are the Confederate quarters'. President Lincoln immediately said, 'I wish to go in here alone!'

I drew myself up into the corner as close as possible, and he bent under the open flap and came in. He went at once to a bedside, and reverently leaned over almost double so low were the cots, and stroked the soldier's head, and with tears streaming down his face he said in a sort of sweet anguish, "Oh, my man, why did you do it?" The boy in gray said, or rather stammered weakly, almost in a whisper, 'I went because my State went'. On that ground floor, so quiet was the whole ward, a pin could almost have been heard to fall. President Lincoln went from one bedside to another and touched each forehead gently, and with tears streaming asked again the question, and again heard the same reply. When he finally passed out from those boys, some grey and grizzled, but many of them children, there came as from one voice, 'Oh, we didn't know he was such a good man! We thought he was a beast!'

At the close of hostilities, I, with many others, went with the army to Richmond and Washington, and there saw the final parade of 60,000 troops before the White House. I afterward returned to my college and hospital and completed my studies, and since then have led a strenuous life as a practising physician in Florida.

As ever,
Your old Comrade,
Mary"

CHAPTER XXVII
Last of City Point

In some early chapters on the good work of the Sanitary Commission I wrote of the denuded hospital camp, belated sick soldiers, etc. After the departure of the Second Corps hospital officers, I was the only white woman in camp, and I took possession of their headquarters, in a rustic cottage of one story built by the engineer corps in pretty artistic style with boughs and branches cut from the woods near by.

MY QUARTERS AT THE CLOSE OF THE WAR

Four rooms, with central entrance, made a comfortable homelike shelter where "Aunty" also stayed and looked after my interests. The colored guard detailed by General Russell marched their steady beat daily and nightly, while a stack of muskets stood before my little door. A circular lawn was often occupied by negroes anxious for a word with "De bressed white Yankee lady," while their picanninies, rolling on the grass, made the place quite lively, despite the warnings of Auntie to "Dem black niggers dat ain't got no manners no-how."

This kind-hearted old mammy always, somehow, managed to have a bright bandanna turban and a fresh white apron. She took that rare possession of me, known only to house servants of southern families.

Mrs. Russell remained in her husband's headquarters at the Point, and afforded me many pleasant social courtesies. General Russell invited me for a buggy ride to Petersburg, still under command of General Willcox.

As we rode by the deserted earthworks and former lines in front of Petersburg,—the field of the last battle being still strewn with empty canteens, broken muskets, etc., its earthworks upturned and great chasms torn as if by an earthquake,—General Russell pointed to a wrecked fort saying "That was the Burnside mine, the 'Crater' where I lost three hundred of the bravest soldiers that ever went into battle. They were the negro hero martyrs of the Burnside mine explosion, where many a brave Yankee white boy also gave up his life."

General Russell's brigade included a number of regiments, among them the Tenth Colored Regiment, with Major William Baker, of Maine, commanding. At the close of the war it was ordered to Texas to subdue the turbulent element and to protect helpless citizens. We met many destitute negroes still flocking to City Point.

As soon as the front lines were abandoned, hundreds of negroes ran from Petersburg to beg our chaplains to marry them. Some were very young; and a grey-haired old man said, "Me and Belinda has just stood by each other ever since we was a'most boy and gall; our chillun is sol' away, and we wants to get married like white folks, so we can't be separated no mo'." This seemed the ultimatum of their understanding of freedom.

Conversions and immersions filled most of their time. These ragged homeless freedmen were gaining some glimmering of morality and religion; but it was a motley crowd that assembled on the shore of the James River, shouting and singing in their childish way, as they were immersed one by one, by their own preacher or leader,—then rising and shouting hallelujahs as they sprang up and down in the water in a frenzied manner, quite ludicrous to observe.

Contrabands were spying out the desolate land, and looking for jobs. Surgeon Thomas Pooley was put in charge of this denuded hospital, and joined my mess in the little cottage where Auntie made some palatable southern dishes with our remaining supplies.

The Christian Commission and State Agencies had "struck their tents" and vanished almost in a night. Happily the Sanitary Commission, with their larger work and supplies, had been detained until the arrival of the stranded regiment, (of which I wrote earlier) when with a detail from General Russell's brigade, still in command of the deserted United States quarters at the Point, they were enabled to reconstruct a sheltered ward into a degree of comfort for the exhausted men. Lack of discipline and policing soon resulted in disorder and untidiness in these formerly perfectly systematized camps. Quantities of unportable home-made furniture, etc., and general debris were left, to the delight of the destitute contrabands. All government tents and property had been "turned in" and strictly registered.

I well remember my farewell glance at the demolished hospital, as I rode for the last time to City Point to take the transport for Washington. Tent roofs gone, only stockade sides remained intact; bunks stripped and bare, much was abandoned that would now be useless to the army. Negroes swarmed like bees around these treasures, and some improvised roofs and shelter from abundant material lying about, and seemed happy in this temporary home with little thought of the future, or knowledge of the Freedmen Bureau then under General Howard's management, devising means to save them from starvation.

I took leave of my faithful, tearful old Auntie, evidently a leader among the irresponsible bewildered contrabands, who felt perfectly happy and safe as long as the Yankees were there to protect them.

At City Point, where little remained to show the old site of General Grant's Headquarters of the United States Armies, as I went aboard a government transport bound for New York,

I showed for the last time my pass, that had given me protection and much independence, and as I look back I am surprised as I think of my perfect freedom from restraint in choosing my patients and my work in the hospital and State Agencies.

As the shore receded, leaving a broken outline of the hospital and Point, a feeling of homesickness, followed by thoughts of trials, discomforts, pleasures, and hopes in our active life among the sick and dying,—as well as the thought of the many recovered and sent home to their friends by army women,—all these passed in kaleidoscopic changes, as, almost alone on board the transport, I turned my face toward Washington, and the months of hospital work waiting for me there. The very last object that attracted my attention, as I looked back, was on a hill just outside the hospital grounds. A great leather army shoe that, on the horizon, looked about the size of a small row boat or canoe, stood out in bold relief. This set me laughing as I remembered the night attempt of the owner to steal from our little house, and the fact that in his flight, months before, he had lost his shoe, not daring to return for it lest he be captured and punished. This monument of his failure remained.

Chapter XXVIII
Washington and New York State Agency

Arrived in Washington I went directly to the home of my army friend, Doctor Hettie K. Painter, to remain until I decided upon my next move. The following day I reported to Colonel Goodrich, head of New York State Agency in Washington, and found that he wished me to remain and assist him in the closing up of the Washington work. This meant the visiting of the several hospitals scattered at long distances over the city and suburbs. Army Square, Douglas and Harewood Hospitals sheltered most of the New York men. I listened to their many complaints at being so long detained when they seemed quite able to travel, but were delayed for various reasons. The work was chiefly of a clerical form, viz.: to find out what difficulties detained the men, and why, when they were entitled to a discharge, it could not be obtained. Some could not get their pay, some had lost their descriptive lists, a few were waiting for their friends to take them home, while still other disabilities interfered.

Owing to the great distances between hospitals which involved a great deal of walking, considerable time was lost and much fatigue followed. I therefore determined to go to Medical Headquarters and ask for an ambulance on the strength of the pass that I still held from General Grant. This authority, of course, was good only during the war, but after some explanations the medical authorities courteously offered to give me the use of a medical headquarters ambulance, though all ambulances had been "called in."

The next morning one came for me, and I was driven to the New York Agency, greatly to the surprise of Colonel Goodrich, who gave me a list of hospital soldiers to visit. At the close of the day I was able to make a complete report. The time saved in driving was considerable, and I was able to accomplish much more than those who had to walk long distances from hospital to hospital, as other agents had then to do.

SERGEANT BOSTON CORBETT

The following day, on calling at the agency for my list, the Colonel said: "Miss Smith, you may visit the near by hospitals to-day, and I will use the ambulance for other work."

"I beg pardon, Colonel," I replied, "I am responsible for the ambulance and no one can use it except by my invitation. If any agent would like to be dropped at any hospital I shall be very happy to accommodate him."

The New York Agency ambulance had been called in, which was rather irritating. The Colonel never quite forgave me this independence, and some time later he remarked, regarding the failure to put through a troublesome case: "Perhaps Miss Smith, with her usual pertinacity, might accomplish it."

"If you can not succeed, Colonel, it is no reason why I should not," I replied quickly. "Please give me the case."

Putting my whole interest and energy into the work, I soon had the satisfaction of reporting the case as settled satisfactorily.

During a visit to Harewood Hospital, I observed a very sleek-looking young man, apparently absorbed in reading the Bible. This man I found was the notorious Boston Corbett who had disobeyed orders to capture Booth alive. He had shot him in the barn, then burning, and which was surrounded by a cordon of troops. For this disobedience Corbett had been imprisoned, but ill-health had brought him to the hospital. I asked him why he had disobeyed orders, and he replied that Booth was about to get away, and he thought it better to shoot him than to run the chance of having him escape. I then asked how he came to have such a remarkable name. He replied: "When I was born my father could not decide upon a name for me, so being a very religious man, he asked the Lord, and the Lord said 'Call him Boston'." I still have the photograph he gave me in his favorite Bible-reading pose.

The piazza of Mrs. Painter's house was separated from that of the adjoining house only by a railing. Here lived a Southern family consisting of father, mother and a beautiful daughter. The father had been secretary to Jefferson Davis, and from a social point of view, was an elegant courteous gentleman. I greatly enjoyed his Southern accent and refined conversation. He had been obliged, through poverty, to rent a part of his house to some Northern politicians.

One day I saw going up the steps, a fine-looking man, Colonel Forney, a prominent politician of that day. He asked politely of this Southern gentleman, then seated on the piazza, if he could see Mr. B., whereupon the owner of the house flew into a rage, as if insulted, and said: "I don't know, suh, ring the bell for the servant!" As the servant opened the door for the Colonel to pass, the irate gentleman said to him, quite childishly,—but in fierce tones,—"Bring me my cut glass carafe of cold water instantly."

A few days later, as we were again sitting on the piazza, having a pleasant chat, this same gentleman told me, with great indignation, of the insults they were now compelled to take from free niggers. He said that a servant maid had become so independent that she would not answer her mistress' bell. "I determined to stop such presumption and ordered my wife to continue ringing while I went down and hid myself behind the kitchen door. The bell rang and rang again while the wench laughed and said to another servant: 'She can just keep on a ringin', an' when I gets good and ready I'll come!' This was too much," he said. "I went quickly forward into the kitchen and slapped her black face twice! The insolent hussy had the temerity to have me hauled to court and bound over to keep the peace!" This was the saddest effect I had yet seen of the influence of slave-holding.

While boarding with Mrs. Painter I met that eccentric yet anomalous woman, Doctor Mary Walker, pleasant, refined and interesting, despite the semi-masculine garb she had then adopted. Her husband, an army surgeon, was, I think, then living, but died soon after the war.

In speaking of her dress, her arguments and logic were unanswerable. She wore loose, long trousers to boot tops, a skirt below her knees, a close-fitting jacket and cape, much like an officer's, high collar and soft hat, all rather becoming for her petite style.

"You," she said, "with long skirts, sweep up and carry home with you samples of all sorts of filth from the streets, and besides you are not modest, for when you must lift your skirts there is always a suggestive display of hosiery, while I go home free from extraneous matter and never have to expose my ankles." This was perfect hygiene and logical; and many times in my army work I wished I could go about without drabbled skirts.

Doctor Walker was, I think, a graduate physician and did much good among sick soldiers. But she gradually grew more pronounced in her mannish attire, and was many times arrested for that infringement of the law. She always pleaded her own case so logically that she was generally dismissed with a reprimand, and cautioned not to do so again. But to this warning she paid no regard; and at one time entered the court-room bearing the United States flag and claiming her rights as an American citizen.

The last I heard of Doctor Mary Walker was from a friend who, in 1908, saw her,—then grown old,—in a Brooklyn car. She was dressed in full male costume,—trousers, collar, tie, dress coat, high silk hat, and held a gaudy little cane.

It was reported that, at a recent Suffrage Convention in Albany, Doctor Walker claimed that New Jersey's early constitution included Women's Suffrage,—that this part of the constitution was never finally repealed, though abrogated in some way, and that therefore New Jersey is a Suffrage State.

CHAPTER XXIX
Old Capitol Prison, Washington D. C., 1865

Among the unusual cases that often fell to me, was that of an elderly man, who had at one time been a judge in New Jersey, but drink had been his undoing. He was now serving a Civil Service sentence for petty larceny in Old Capitol Prison. I saw at once that he was a "bummer," but that he had been a gentleman while sober. I did not feel much interest in this man personally, but he showed me a letter from his son, evidently educated, in which he begged his father to come home, saying he would take care of him and they might live together and be happy. The man had been a soldier for a short time, but had been degraded and discharged, and was now a prisoner of Civil Law. It was a difficult case, but for the sake of his faithful son I undertook it. I went to Judge Carter, of that district, urging him to let the man go.

"It is of no use, Miss Smith. The old fellow is a scamp and not to be trusted for a moment," was the reply. "He will steal anything, and if I should let him go to-day he would be back here to-morrow on another charge. He was arrested on the charge of stealing a wheel-barrow."

"Why, Judge," I said, laughing, "he did not know what he was doing. He might as well have stolen a grindstone!"

This seemed greatly to amuse the judge, and he said directly: "Well, that settles it; if you will see that he goes out of the city on the train to his son, he may go. If he gets free he will be back here in a week on another charge."

Quite pleased with my success, I went to the Sanitary Commission, still in Washington, secured a ticket to his home, and wrote to his son to meet him; then I notified the old man to be ready at a certain hour the next day when I would call for him.

When I went to the prison for him he began a round of deliberate lying, and tried every subterfuge to evade me and get away, so that he might remain in Washington. Finally I said: "You will go with me to the train where I will put you in charge of the conductor, who will deliver you to your son, and if you will not agree to this you may remain where you are."

GENERAL WINFIELD SCOTT HANCOCK

At last we started on our way down Pennsylvania Avenue. He insisted that the Government owed him money, so I took him to General Brice's office, where his clerks soon found a record of desertion, fraud, and bounty-jumping. I lost no time in getting him to the train, threatening to have him arrested if he attempted to give me the slip. The conductor took him in charge and promised to deliver him to his son, and I was glad to get the old sinner off my hands. A few days after, I received a grateful letter from the faithful son.

Some months later I chanced to see a Jersey paper which stated that my old scamp had been arrested for stealing photograph albums, and that he had formerly been a reputable judge.

On returning from the train I stopped at the War Department for advice in some other cases. There I chanced to meet General Winfield Hancock, who gave me his autograph, and, chatting easily, we walked up Pennsylvania Avenue. And so it happened that I had walked down Pennsylvania Avenue with a miserable old "prison bird" and had walked up the Avenue with "the handsomest man in the army," whose appearance was greatly enhanced by a spotless, brilliant uniform.

At Army Square Hospital I met again my former patient of City Point, who had captured his young rebel brother, the Captain. Their faithful brother had, with much care and difficulty, succeeded in bringing them to this hospital, but the cheerful young captain had died there from gangrene,— perhaps due to carelessness. The Major, weaker than when at City Point, unable to speak, motioned his brother to say that he had not forgotten the Lincoln badge I had given him, and that he would always cherish it. His devoted brother had struggled heroically to reach their city, and the Major had at least his wish to die at home. Thus ended another of the many tragedies of our unholy, unnecessary war.

During my last weeks in Washington, I attended a session of the trial of Wirz, a Swiss, formerly turnkey of Andersonville prison, who was later found guilty of barbarous treatment of prisoners of war and condemned to be hanged, with eight conspirators against the life of President Lincoln, including Mrs. Surette. I believe, however, that only four, including Mrs. Surette, were executed. These were the only traitors that suffered ignominious death. Can any other victorious nation show such Christian clemency?

Assisted by the Agency and Government Departments, I had great success in difficult cases. After much travelling about from one department to another in the interest of a convalescent soldier, I collected for him fifty dollars,—which was long due, and which at once enabled him to start for his home, greatly elated by his freedom.

An erratic, wild Irishman was made almost delirious by getting his long delayed three hundred dollars, and insisted upon giving me fifty dollars of it, but I informed him that I did not work for pay. He wrote me from New York later, on a double sheet of cap, in letters an inch long, with "God bless you!" scrawled all over the page.

Having left Doctor Painter's hospitable home, I was now boarding on K Street, where I met a most charming blonde Scotch girl—Cordelia Anderson, holding a responsible position in the Treasury Department. She made my evenings delightful, as had my friend Annie Bain in our field tent at City Point, after the strain, the work and indignation of almost every day. A few years later, this rare young woman, still in Washington in July of '67, sent for me to come to her on my way north on my vacation from Norfolk, Virginia, where I was Superintendent of Colored Schools. She was very ill with typhoid. I nursed her till the doctor insisted that for my own health I must leave her, when a kindly old Auntie took charge until her recovery.

The intolerable heat of Washington at that season was unusual. The streets were not paved, and a fine impalpable dust, continually rising, was suffocating. At the boarding house where we were, I saw the most astonishing rats, as large as small cats; and at night when I went down-stairs to get ice for the sick girl, they ran up-stairs ahead of me, and coolly sat upon their haunches, blinking at me with their vicious black eyes.

CORDELIA ANDERSON

CHAPTER XXX
The Last Act in My Drama at Washington

While still working at high tension I suddenly became aware that even my great vitality and good health demanded a rest, and I was preparing to leave for home, when Mr. Huron, of the Indiana State Agency, who had nearly lost his pretty wife by typhoid at City Point, came urging me to undertake an unusually difficult case, an application for discharge. I insisted that I had not enough energy left to win another case. His discharge had been repeatedly blocked, even though urged by the Secretary of the State of Indiana, and there seemed to be no hope of sending this brave soldier home. However, Mr. Huron's statement of injustice was so exasperating that, in righteous indignation, I determined to remain and make one more effort at this last moment. This man, who had served his full term of four years honorably, and had lost a leg, was, without consent, placed on the roll of the Invalid Corps, which indignity old soldiers considered a stain on their army escutcheon. Many appeals had failed to accomplish his discharge. The case was always "referred back" to the hospital where it was duly "pigeon-holed." The man's sister had come to Washington expecting to take him home to Indiana, but for weeks all their efforts had failed, and now some legal complications had culminated which required his presence at home to save their little property and farm.

The next day I went to the hospital, and after listening to the man's statement I went directly to the surgeon in charge, and stated the case,—to which he replied with some discourtesy. Having received the utmost courtesy and respect and attention from all the departments when I had asked for help, my temper rose to the occasion when he said: "The man has no descriptive list, and I will attend to it when I think best!"

"That will not answer my purpose," I replied warmly. "I wish the man to go at once!" and I made some strong statements of the urgency of the situation. He assumed a dignified silence; on which I stated emphatically "The man is going! If you do not help me in the matter, he will go just the same!" My indignation was then sufficient to put through a half dozen cases.

Going directly to the Medical Department, I made known to Surgeons Middletown and Abbott the unjust detention of this loyal soldier. They had always promptly aided me in other cases; and upon hearing my statement they also became indignant, and offered me every help. I had "turned in" my ambulance with many thanks, when I intended to leave for home; but Doctor Middletown said "You had better have our headquarters' ambulance, for you have many miles to travel over the city to put this matter through, and I will go 'over the head' of this surgeon and order him to order a descriptive list."

With this document I was much encouraged, and went next morning to the hospital and my aristocratic surgeon, who tried not to appear surprised as he said loftily: "I will attend to it."

"Excuse me," I said, "I came directly from Headquarters to get your signature, and to deliver the paper to the Medical Department myself."

He dared not refuse this order, and sent for the steward and gave him the paper to fill out the order. I followed closely on the heels of this man to his office, where he coolly thrust the paper into a pigeon-hole and sat down. Surmising that his intention was to make me wait until after office hours, I at last said to him: "Steward, if you do not intend to make out that paper at once I shall report you to Medical Headquarters." He soon found time and made out the paper, and I rode away to unravel more red tape. At the Medical Department the doctors signed the paper, and directed me to take it to the War Department. Distances were great and office hours short, and so another day passed. But at the earliest moment on the following day, we drove to the War

Department, where I found Captain Sam Breck, now a retired General, a handsome thoroughbred gentleman who had done me many army favors.

"Why, Miss Smith," he exclaimed cheerfully, "are you here yet? I thought you were through with us."

"Well, Captain, you haven't got rid of me yet, and though I am completely tired out, I have taken another most distressing case, and I'm going to sit right down here and talk until you help me out."

Jokingly, he said, "Oh, I can't stand that, so let us see if I can save your breath."

I stated the case as briefly as possible, and his sense of justice was aroused as he said emphatically, "I will help you with this case."

"How long does it take to put through a descriptive list?" I asked.

"Well," he replied, "about three weeks usually!"

"Oh," I exclaimed, "that won't do. I can't stay so long, and if I leave the papers they'll be pigeon-holed again."

He thought a moment, and said, "Let me have the papers," and he left me waiting in his office.

On returning the paper he said, "There, Miss Smith, that has never before been done in this Department. The descriptive list has been put through in fifteen minutes. Take it to your doctor, and he will be obliged to sign it; and then your man will be free."

Too delighted and relieved to properly express my thanks, I said—"Good-bye for good this time, Captain. I promise not to trouble you any more!"

Again in the ambulance I said to the driver, who was very much interested, "Now, Orderly, your horses can not go too fast for me!" and soon we dashed up to the hospital grounds.

Meanwhile the case had become hospital gossip, and every "Boy" knew of my work. The doctor gave me the slip, but I followed him up through the wards till I found him at last in his office. In passing through the wards I waved the paper saying—"Boys, I have it, I have it!" A low cheer passed round as the good news spread from ward to ward.

On presenting this order I said, "Doctor, will you please sign this?"

With an effort he controlled his expression, and said quite blandly, "Er, er—when would you like to have this man go?"

"Immediately, if you please!"—with extreme politeness.

"Oh! then I will order the ambulance."

"Thank you," I replied, "I have the Medical Headquarters' Ambulance waiting and will take the man with me just as soon as he can be made ready." I then bowed myself out politely.

In half an hour the happy cripple was placed beside me in the ambulance, and we drove directly to Mr. Huron's home, where the now rejoicing sister was waiting. She started at once to take her brother home by easy stages, and we heard that they had reached their little farm in safety. A letter of appreciation from the Secretary of the State of Indiana was a satisfactory ending to this almost impossible case.

In my many visits to this hospital I had discovered some "irregularities," for instance, that a number of soldiers were detained on various pretexts in order that the requisite number might be maintained, with their "rations" (thirty-seven cents per diem) to keep open this hospital. So many men begged me, almost upon their knees, to help them. As this was quite beyond my strength I resolved to report the matter to General Grant's headquarters. During my call he listened politely and silently, laid away his cigar, gave me his attention, and referred me to Adjutant Bowers, who exclaimed: "Why, that is impossible! Here is an order sent some weeks ago directing all convalescents to be discharged at once!"

"Nevertheless, Colonel," I replied, "the men remain."

With some excitement he replied, "If you can get me the names of these men, and I find that orders have not been followed, I will close that hospital, at once."

This decision and the fact that General Grant had given me his autograph during my visit, made me very happy. I diplomatically secured a list of about twenty men who were being wrongfully detained, and this was at once conveyed to Colonel Bowers. This was my "Coup d' état" in Washington; and I thought it a good time to retire from hospital work and to return to my home for rest. Two weeks later I saw by a

Washington paper that all patients at this hospital able to travel had been sent home, and a small remainder of those still sick had been carried to Harewood Hospital, the former hospital having ended its career.

I had hoped to meet General Grant's Military Secretary, General Eli Parker, who wrote the draft of the surrender of Appomattox. He was said to have been of imposing appearance. He was chief of the Senecas and of the Six Nations, and his Indian name was Donehogawa. When at home on their reservation with their father, his sisters, who, when in Washington, were among the cultured society of the Capitol, wore the rich costumes of princesses of the tribe and were treated with the homage due to their rank.

Thus ended my work in Washington for the "Boys in Blue."

Chapter XXXI
Transportation Home

The war was over, and government passes and government roads were of the past, only regular army transportation was now allowed, except to the Medical Department for the purpose of sending home delayed patients. My "Grant Pass," that had made me so independent, became at once only a relic. Therefore, being entitled to transportation to my home, I went to Surgeon General Barnes, U. S. A., to receive that privilege. After a pleasant conversation with the General, he remarked, "Your name is not on the pay roll, and you are entitled to pay for army service. If you will make out your claim I will endorse it."

To this I replied,—with more sentiment, as I now see it, than judgment,—"General, I thank you, but I do not wish pay for my services in hospital work. If I had been a man I would have enlisted as a soldier. But being only a woman it was all I could do, and I wish to give that service to my country."

Often, since then, I have thought of the quizzical expression of the General's eyes, though he said not a word about an impractical girl who did not think far enough to see what good she might have done with that accumulated wage of several years.

At that time, however, I was receiving (during several months) sixty dollars per month as New York State Agent,— the only pay I ever received. But that seemed different. The war was over.

The General then asked how far I wanted transportation. I replied that I lived in Brooklyn, but would take transportation as far as he would give it. But as I used it only to my home I still have the following form of transportation:

"Boston & Maine R. R.
This Order not Transferable.
D. No. 51978
Oct. 20, 1865.
Transport Miss Ada W. Smith
From Boston, Mass., to Portland, Me.
En Route from Washington to Augusta, Me.
Signature of officer issuing the order,
IRA G. PAYNE,
Capt. A. Q. M.
By order of the Quarter Master General,
LEWIS B. PARSONS,
Col. & Chief of Rail and River Transportation."

Resting only a few days after my return to my home, I was urged by friends on the Sanitary Commission to assist, with another, a lady of remarkable ability, a Miss Baldwin, in dispensing some surplus funds for the Sanitary Commission, with Headquarters in New York City. This surplus could not, according to their organization, be used for other purposes than for the benefit of soldiers. After much discussion it seemed that the soldiers' families should be the natural recipients. So during most of that unusually severe winter, 1865-6, I went daily from my home in Brooklyn to New York, and with my companion found many families in need of help, who might otherwise have perished with cold. When spring brought relief, the last dollar of that grand life-saving organization was expended.

This was, of course, before the day of pensions. We continued this work until the funds were exhausted. Then I retired finally from the engrossing activity of hospital life and caring for soldiers' families, in which I was engaged from 1862 through 1866.

I had been very happy in this ministration that daily brought its reward in the gratitude and appreciation of my "Boys in Blue," and in the thought that I had done at least what I could in that fearful struggle to save our Union and glorious country.

No one really desires to grow old, but I would not have missed that call for every heart and hand to respond to its duty, even to be young again.

> And the star spangled banner
> In triumph shall wave,
> O'er the land of the free
> And the home of the brave.
>
> Francis Scott Key

ADELAIDE W. SMITH, 1867

Adjutant Wm. J. Harding
Commander E.A. Cruikshank
Quartermaster Henry A. Cozzens
Headquarters   U.S. Grant   Post No. 327
Department of New York. Grand Army of the Republic.
489 Washington Avenue
Telephone: Prospect 546, Brooklyn, July 15, 1909

MISS ADELAIDE W. SMITH gave her lecture, "Hospital Experience During the War," before the U. S. Grant Post of Brooklyn, on Tuesday evening, March 9th last, under the auspices of the Entertainment Committee. A large audience was present to greet Miss Smith. The subject, itself one of absorbing interest, was skilfully presented by the lecturer and was received with marked attention and interest.

I take very great pleasure in commending Miss Smith's

lecture to the G. A. R. Posts of New York and vicinity also to Church Societies, Clubs, Schools, and other organizations that go to make up the social and intellectual life of a community. Miss Smith's services to our sick and wounded soldiers from 1861 to 1865 entitle her to the generous recognition of our comrades, and the men and women of America.

(Signed) ANDREW JACOBS,
Chairman Entertainment Committee,
U. S. Grant Post,
Brooklyn, New York

www.ingramcontent.com/pod-product-compliance
Lightning Source LLC
Chambersburg PA
CBHW020918160726
47993CB00005B/2026